Wordly Wise

Kenneth Hodkinson

BOOK 6

Revised

EDUCATORS PUBLISHING SERVICE
Cambridge and Toronto

Cover Design: Huge Price

Printed in USA

ISBN 978-0-8388-0436-0

10 11 12 13 PAH 12 11 10

Contents

WORD LIST v
INTRODUCTION vii

CHAPTER ONE
    Word List – Lesson 1 1
    Word List – Lesson 2 7
    Word List – Lesson 3 13
    Chapter One Crossword Puzzle 19

CHAPTER TWO
    Word List – Lesson 4 20
    Word List – Lesson 5 25
    Word List – Lesson 6 31
    Chapter Two Crossword Puzzle 38

CHAPTER THREE
    Word List – Lesson 7 39
    Word List – Lesson 8 45
    Word List – Lesson 9 50
    Chapter Three Crossword Puzzle 56

CHAPTER FOUR
    Word List – Lesson 10 57
    Word List – Lesson 11 63
    Word List – Lesson 12 68
    Chapter Four Crossword Puzzle 75

CHAPTER FIVE
    Word List – Lesson 13 76
    Word List – Lesson 14 81
    Word List – Lesson 15 87
    Chapter Five Crossword Puzzle 93

CHAPTER SIX
    Word List – Lesson 16 94
    Word List – Lesson 17 99
    Word List – Lesson 18 105
    Chapter Six Crossword Puzzle 111

CHAPTER SEVEN
    Word List – Lesson 19 112
    Word List – Lesson 20 117
    Word List – Lesson 21 122
    Chapter Seven Crossword Puzzle 128

CHAPTER EIGHT
    Word List – Lesson 22 129
    Word List – Lesson 23 134
    Word List – Lesson 24 139
    Chapter Eight Crossword Puzzle 146

Word List

(Numbers in parentheses refer to the Word List in which the word appears.)

ABBREVIATED (10)

abet (4)
abnormal (13)
abridged (7)
abstinence (19)
abstract (6)
accord (4)
accumulate (22)
acidulous (16)
acquiesce (10)
acrid (7)
adept (6)
adjunct (20)
administer (17)
advent (18)
aegis (3)
aftermath (1)
alumni (8)
amble (24)
amorous (11)
amphibian (8)
amputate (24)
annex (7)
annotated (9)
anticlimax (21)
antipodes (1)
antithesis (6)
appalled (18)
apparition (12)
appraise (9)
aptitude (15)
aqueduct (2)
aquiline (17)
arbitrary (8)
assiduous (10)
astral (15)
attest (16)
averse (5)
awl (4)

BADGER (23)

baleful (14)
balk (22)
bandy (8)
beguile (22)
benevolent (19)

betrothed (6)
binocular (7)
bleak (13)
budget (3)
buffoon (19)
bulwark (9)

CARAVAN (2)

caries (3)
carnage (7)
census (5)
chaos (11)
chasten (9)
chastise (2)
chicanery (19)
choleric (20)
chronicle (3)
cleric (17)
cloister (12)
coerce (4)
combine (11)
compassion (22)
conifer (9)
conscientious (21)
consecutive (13)
conserve (9)
contagious (20)
contravene (22)
contrite (4)
conversant (15)
copious (6)
counterfeit (12)
countermand (21)
craven (18)
credence (8)
credulous (6)
cull (8)

DATA (7)

decipher (1)
deem (3)
degrading (1)
dehydrate (17)
deity (22)
dell (17)

delta (12)
demean (2)
demeanor (11)
demented (6)
demise (14)
denizen (19)
detract (10)
devious (16)
dialogue (3)
diction (15)
dilate (18)
disclaim (5)
distend (7)
divulge (11)
doughty (13)
dregs (24)
duress (23)

EARTHY (6)

eccentric (6)
edifying (2)
efface (13)
elicit (2)
elite (1)
ellipse (20)
ellipsis (15)
elocution (17)
emanate (20)
embellish (9)
enclosure (10)
encompass (23)
engrave (3)
ennui (13)
ensure (16)
envoy (17)
ephemeral (11)
epistle (7)
epitome (11)
eschew (10)
ethereal (18)
euphoria (14)
evince (20)
ewer (3)
exact (22)
exemplify (18)
exhilarating (2)

exorbitant (8)
exterminate (5)
extinguish (21)
extricate (24)
exude (23)

FABULOUS (3)

factotum (7)
fallible (16)
farrier (2)
feasible (20)
flaccid (23)
flay (7)
fluent (12)
fodder (4)
foretell (13)
format (23)
furor (19)
futile (14)

GALAXY (1)

gaudy (16)
gauntlet (13)
genius (2)
gig (3)
gingerly (12)
gird (2)
glean (19)
gloss (20)
gorge (11)
grotto (7)
guile (17)
gullible (8)
guttural (11)

HACKNEYED (14)

hazy (1)
hemorrhage (5)
heretic (12)
heterodox (13)
hidebound (9)
hilt (11)
historic (3)
humdrum (15)
hydraulic (21)
hypothetical (3)

IDOLATRY (16)

illicit (24)
illiterate (18)
immaculate (23)
immobile (22)
impart (10)
impassive (9)
impel (17)
implication (21)
impostor (17)
inaugurate (9)
incarcerate (24)
incision (24)
incongruous (13)
incorrigible (4)
inexorable (5)
inexplicable (1)
ingenious (21)
insight (4)
inter (2)
interrogate (2)
intrepid (8)
invincible (17)
iota (23)
irony (15)
irrelevant (16)

JIG (21)

LATENT (14)

lateral (18)
leach (16)
lineament (22)
lissome (18)
lucrative (12)
lucre (3)
lunar (17)

MAGNANIMOUS (23)

malingerer (14)
mannerism (10)
martyr (12)

massacre (19)
meditate (16)
meticulous (20)
migratory (17)
mimic (11)
minimize (19)
misanthrope (15)
miscreant (21)
moccasin (4)
myriad (13)

NEBULOUS (10)
nominal (15)
noncommittal (16)
noxious (24)

OBESE (14)
odometer (18)
odorous (3)
omniscient (15)
ordnance (17)
orgy (13)
osier (15)
ottoman (20)
oust (4)
overseer (7)

PANDER (8)
papyrus (19)
paramount (11)
paraphernalia (1)
pedantic (23)
penance (18)
pendulous (24)
pervade (9)

pestilence (4)
pewter (18)
pious (12)
pithy (14)
plagiarism (22)
plaudit (1)
plight (23)
porous (15)
portage (22)
portcullis (11)
posterity (21)
posthumous (1)
prate (19)
pretentious (21)
prevalent (15)
primitive (2)
profess (21)
prolific (16)
prone (18)
protégé (23)
provisional (24)
prudent (12)
pseudonym (23)
pugnacious (2)

QUAIL (1)

RANGY (18)
rank (2)
rarity (3)
recoil (10)
recompense (16)
regimen (16)
remit (6)
remonstrate (1)

remuneration (10)
replenish (11)
reprehensible (8)
repudiate (4)
reputable (5)
rescind (17)
restitution (8)
resurgent (8)
reverent (4)
rigorous (11)
rime (10)
roisterer (5)
rote (1)

SAGE (4)
saline (20)
sanctum (18)
satiety (24)
saturate (15)
scribe (19)
secede (22)
sedate (23)
senile (22)
sensuous (12)
sepulcher (6)
sere (15)
silo (14)
simile (6)
sinister (3)
skimp (9)
sleazy (6)
snub (12)
solar (13)
spasm (24)
spawn (5)

specific (24)
specify (1)
squeamish (7)
stalwart (9)
stenographer (18)
stilted (9)
stipulate (5)
suave (10)
surplus (5)
surreptitious (14)
sustenance (22)
symbol (7)
synthesis (21)
synthetic (6)

TABOO (19)
tacit (19)
tangible (5)
tantalize (20)
tempo (6)
temporal (11)
tenacious (23)
tenuous (21)
testimony (14)
textile (4)
thwart (13)
titanic (16)
titillate (8)
toga (5)
tonic (14)
torpid (12)
totalitarian (24)
tourniquet (14)
tractable (14)
trait (24)

trance (5)
transcribe (7)
transient (13)
transpose (8)
treatise (9)
triad (3)
tribunal (20)
turgid (22)

UMBRAGE (4)
unassuming (1)
uncouth (14)
undoing (12)
undulate (6)
usury (15)

VEHEMENT (20)
veneer (17)
vigilante (5)
vindictive (5)
virulent (10)
void (19)
vouch (12)

WEND (2)
wraith (16)
writ (10)
wry (18)

YOKEL (13)

ZONE (1)

Introduction

This book has four main purposes: (1) to help you learn new words, (2) to give you a better understanding of how words are formed and how they are used, (3) to give you some idea of where many of our words come from and some of the interesting stories behind them, and (4) perhaps most important from your point of view, to make the learning of this material interesting and enjoyable.

Here are a few tips to help you get the most out of the book:

Keep a dictionary close at hand as you do the exercises. You will need one that gives word origins. *Webster's New World Dictionary* in the Popular Library pocket-sized edition is recommended because it contains this information and is also quite inexpensive.

Make use of the Wordly Wise section which you will find at the end of most lessons. You may need to refer to this section while doing some of the exercises, so it is a good idea to read the section over thoroughly at the start of each lesson.

Remember that many words have more than one meaning. Don't be satisfied until you know *all* the meanings of a word and can use the word freely and comfortably. There are five exercises in each lesson; don't skip any of them.

The format of this book has been kept simple. The five exercises in each lesson are headed A, B, C, D, and E. All the A exercises are done in the same way; all the B exercises are done in the same way, and so on.

After each set of three lessons, there is a crossword puzzle which uses all the words you have learned in those three lessons. This review will help refresh your memory.

Certain terms are used in this book, and you should be thoroughly familiar with their meanings. These terms are as follows:

Synonym
A synonym is a word having the same or nearly the same meaning as another word in the same language. *Small* and *little* are synonyms, so are *talk* and *speak*.

Antonym
An antonym is a word having an opposite meaning to another word. *Up* and *down* are antonyms, so are *sad* and *happy*.

Homonym
A homonym is a word having the same pronunciation as another word but a different meaning and usually a different spelling. *Coarse* and *course* are homonyms, so are *bare* and *bear*.

Root
A root is a word or part of a word that is used as a base on which to make other words. The word *body* is a root since we can make such new words as *embody, disembodied, bodily* from it. *Ept* is a root, although it is not a word, because from it we can make such words as *adept* and *inept*.

Prefix
A prefix is a syllable or a group of syllables attached to the beginning of a word to change its meaning. Some common prefixes are *un-, non-, re-,* and *anti-*. Some others already mentioned in the above entry on roots are *em-, dis-, ad-,* and *in-*. Most of our prefixes have come to us from Greek or Latin.

Suffix
A suffix is a syllable or a group of syllables attached to the end of a word to change its meaning. Some common suffixes are *-ness, -ed, -er, -ly,* and *-able*. Many of our suffixes have come to us from Greek or Latin.

Let us put a root, suffix, and prefix together in an example. By adding the suffix -*ful* to the root *help*, we get the adjective *helpful*, which means "of service or assistance." We can add a prefix *un-*, which means "not," and form a new adjective, *unhelpful*, which means "not helpful."

If you come upon any of the above terms while working on the exercises in this book and are not sure of their meanings, turn back to the entries above.

Chapter One

Word List 1

AFTERMATH	HAZY	REMONSTRATE
ANTIPODES	INEXPLICABLE	ROTE
DECIPHER	PARAPHERNALIA	SPECIFY
DEGRADING	PLAUDIT	UNASSUMING
ELITE	POSTHUMOUS	ZONE
GALAXY	QUAIL	

Look up the words above in your dictionary. Note that some of the words have more than one meaning. When you feel that you know *all* the meanings of *all* the words, go on to the exercise below.

EXERCISE 1A

From the four choices under each phrase or sentence, you are to mark the one that is closest in meaning to the word appearing in italics. When the same word appears more than once, you should note that it is being used in a different sense.

1. a lot of *paraphernalia*
   (a) useless argument (b) personal belongings (c) legal maneuvering (d) organized activity

2. the *aftermath* of the hurricane
   (a) cost (b) cause (c) consequence (d) uselessness

3. *hazy* ideas
   (a) ambitious (b) unclear (c) clever (d) practical

4. a slight *haze*
   (a) eruption of the skin (b) lack of clearness in the air (c) case of mistaken identity (d) defect in a person's eyesight

5. a no-parking *zone*
   (a) injury (b) scare (c) situation (d) area

6. to study the *galaxy*
   (a) arrangement of particles in an atom (b) group of vast numbers of stars (c) depths of the ocean (d) sun's planets taken as a group

7. a *galaxy* of prominent world leaders
   (a) large wall painting (b) distinguished gathering (c) historical study (d) confidential adviser

8. learning by *rote*
   (a) following the example of others (b) thinking for oneself (c) memorizing in an unthinking way (d) reading quietly to oneself

9. an *unassuming* manner
   (a) modest (b) suspicious (c) proud (d) deceptive

10. to visit the *antipodes*
    (a) chain of volcanic mountains (b) chain of islands formed of coral (c) region around the equator (d) region on the opposite side of the world

11. to *decipher* coded messages
    (a) make up (b) translate into ordinary language (c) be baffled by (d) transmit by wireless

12. to *decipher* the meaning
    (a) change (b) hide (c) figure out (d) fail to understand

13. *inexplicable* behavior
    (a) incapable of being explained (b) incapable of being excused (c) contrary to the law (d) absurdly comical

14. to *remonstrate*
    (a) remain silent (b) speak in sign language
    (c) speak in protest (d) speak pleadingly

15. to *quail*
    (a) make a low wailing sound (b) haggle over the price (c) engage in argument (d) draw back in fear

16. a young *quail*
    (a) transplanted tree or bush (b) small game bird (c) apprentice sailor (d) cowardly child

17. a member of an *elite*
    (a) secret society (b) superior group (c) society promoting self-help (d) inferior group

18. *degrading* treatment
    (a) of extended duration (b) lowering in self respect (c) beneficial to one's health (d) just and impartial

19. the *plaudits* of the crowd
    (a) particular favorites (b) expressions of displeasure (c) peculiar characteristics (d) expressions of approval

20. the writer's *posthumous* fame
    (a) occurring after her death (b) undeserved (c) richly deserved (d) occurring in her lifetime

21. to *specify* a time
    (a) object to (b) state definitely (c) set aside (d) extend

22. to *specify* teakwood
    (a) import (b) call for explicitly (c) export (d) make do with

Check your answers against the correct ones at the top of the next column. The answers are not in order; this is to prevent your eye from catching sight of the correct ones before you have had a chance to do the exercise on your own.

17b. 3b. 7b. 6b. 12c. 19d. 2c. 20a. 11b. 22b. 1b. 15d. 10d. 5d. 16b. 21b. 18b. 8c. 14c. 4b. 13a. 9a.

Go back to your dictionary and look up again those words for which you gave incorrect answers. Only after doing this should you go on to the next exercise.

EXERCISE 1B

Each word in Word List 1 is used four times in the sentences below; one of the sentences in each group uses the word incorrectly. You are to circle the letter that precedes that sentence. Do not circle more than one letter in any one group.

1. (a) Visibility was no more than two or three miles because of the *haze*. (b) He gave a somewhat *hazy* account of where he had been. (c) The doctor thought that glasses would help the woman's *hazy* eyesight. (d) She has only the *haziest* idea what subjects to take in college.

2. (a) The children repeated by *rote* the things they had learned. (b) Learning by *rote* does not encourage independent thinking. (c) Everything was done by *rote* there, and a person who thought for himself would have been a misfit. (d) The children tried to *rote* into their minds the names of all the presidents.

3. (a) The message was written in a *decipher* that no one could understand. (b) Her handwriting is so poor that I cannot *decipher* what she wrote. (c) Since the postmark was smudged, we were unable to *decipher* the name of the town where the letter had been mailed. (d) The message was in code, but I quickly *deciphered* it.

4. (a) She *remonstrated* with her brother for his refusal to take part in the game. (b) They ignored the *remonstrances* of friends and did exactly as they pleased. (c) She *remonstrated* a strong desire for an education by studying during the day and working at night. (d) The decision of the referee caused the crowd to *remonstrate* violently with him.

5. (a) She didn't *specify* any particular time for me to call her. (b) With her telescope she was able to *specify* something moving among the trees. (c) The architect *specified* stainless steel for all the kitchen fixtures. (d) I have checked the *specifications* for the building, and they do call for oak floors.

6. (a) Laden with fishing *paraphernalia*, the two men mad their way to the river. (b) Each man was given a *paraphernalia* before setting out. (c) His baseball *paraphernalia* was scattered all over the room. (d) it was an incredible feat to move fifty scientists with all the *paraphernalia* of a geological survey across the mountains.

7. (a) **The sun is simply one of millions of stars that make up our** *galaxy*. (b) **The club holds a** *galaxy* **for the children every Christmas.** (c) **I was overwhelmed at being asked to address such a** *galaxy* **of distinguished scientists.** (d) **Inter-***galactic* **space travel may be possible in the very distant future.**

8. (a) She is so *unassuming* that you would never guess her to be the president of the company. (b) His quiet, *unassuming* ways endeared him to his fellow workers. (c) I joined the actors as they were *unassuming* their costumes. (d) She gave instructions so *unassumingly* that no one took offense.

9. (a) Many parents find the behavior of their teenage children *inexplicable*. (b) The ball of yarn was completely *inexplicable* after the cat had finished playing with it. (c) The disappearance of everyone connected with the case has presented the police with an *inexplicable* mystery. (d) She *inexplicably* failed to collect the money I was holding for her.

10. (a) He had to *elite* several passages from his speech because it was much too long. (b) **The people who live on the hill consider themselves the** *elite* **of the town.** (c) **The Prussian officers were the** *elite* **of the German army.** (d) **A scientific** *elite* **is making its presence felt in this country.**

11. (a) His voice became slightly *posthumous* as he spoke of those far off days. (b) A *posthumous* child is one born after the death of the mother. (c) He was completely unknown when he died, and his fame has been entirely *posthumous*. (d) Ernest Hemingway's **A Moveable Feast** was published *posthumously* from papers collected by his widow.

12. (a) Aspirin relieves headaches and has no harmful *aftermaths*. (b) The dislocation in world trade was an *aftermath* of the political instability. (c) The backache he complains of is an *aftermath* of the accident. (d) The spread of typhoid fever throughout the region is the *aftermath* of the earthquake.

13. (a) This part of the town is *zoned* for light industry. (b) I *zoned* over as quickly as I could when I heard what had happened. (c) The world is divided into five *zones*, named according to the general climate of each. (d) Cities are divided into postal *zones* to make the delivery of mail easier.

14. (a) In the early nineteenth century, convicts from Britain were sent out to the *Antipodes*. (b) What she claimed I said was the complete *antipodes* of what I actually said. (c) The British refer to Australia and New Zealand as the *Antipodes*. (d) To a person at the North Pole, the *antipodes* would be the South Pole.

15. (a) Armed soldiers were called out to *quail* the rebellion. (b) They loved life and embraced it fiercely but did not *quail* at the thought of death. (c) The *quail* is similar to, but is smaller than, the partridge. (d) The strongest men *quailed* before her, so terrible was her rage.

16. (a) She had been trained as an engineer and found it *degrading* to work as a road sweeper. (b) He was *degrading* the eggs into different sizes when I walked in. (c) She claimed that war, far from being noble, was *degrading* and hateful. (d) The inmates revolted against the *degrading* conditions in the prison.

17. (a) With the *plaudits* of the crowd ringing in her ears, she retired from the stage. (b) She thought poorly of her book, so she was astonished by the *plaudits* of the critics. (c) She sent him a *plaudit* expressing her thanks for his fine performance. (d) As an actor he was insecure and needed the *plaudits* of the crowd.

EXERCISE 1C

Rewrite each of the sentences below, replacing the italicized word or phrase with a word from Word List 1 and writing the word in the form that fits the rest of the sentence. Use each word only once. Write your answers in the spaces provided.

1. She took a lot of *personal belongings* with her on her trip to the *other side of the world*.

   . . . .

   . . . .

2. He lived through the *unpleasant events that were the result* of the war, but his memory of those days is *blurred and indistinct*.

   . . . .

   . . . .

3. Students learn by *a fixed, mechanical repetition* how to *translate into everyday language* the coded messages that are received.

   . . . .

   . . . .

4. She is so *lacking in boldness* that she didn't even *state definitely* the method she wanted us to use.

   . . . .

   . . . .

5. The novel was published *after the death of the author* and received the *admiring expressions of approval* of the critics.

   . . . .

   . . . .

6. It is *lowering to one's dignity* to have to admit that one is not a member of the *group that is considered superior*.

   . . . .

   . . . .

7. He *drew back in fear* when I began to *speak in a harsh and critical manner* with him.

   . . . .

   . . . .

8. This *vast number of stars, taken as a group,* may contain millions of planets like our earth.

   . . . .

   . . . .

9. The reason for the change in climate from one *region of the earth* to another is *incapable of being explained* to me.

   . . . .

   . . . .

EXERCISE 1D

The following questions deal with prefixes, roots, and suffixes. If you are not sure what is meant by these terms, you should turn back to the Introduction, where you will find them explained.

In- is a Latin prefix meaning "not" or "opposite to"; thus, INEXPLICABLE is opposite in meaning to *explicable*. Other Latin prefixes with this same meaning are *dis-*, *un-*, and *non-*. Note also that *in-* becomes *im-* before *b, m,* and *p; il-* before *l;* and *ir-* before *r.*

For each word below, write the word opposite in meaning by using the appropriate prefix.

1. comfort . . . .

2. comfortable . . . .

3. discreet . . . .

4. sense . . . .

5. finite . . . .

6. legible . . . .

7. arm (verb) . . . .

8. armed (adjective) . . . .

9. responsible . . . .

10. legal . . . .

11. moderate . . . .

12. mature . . . .

Explain the difference in meaning between the following pairs of words.

13. *disinterested* and *uninterested*

. . . .

. . . .

14. *disqualified* and *unqualified*

. . . .

. . . .

15. *nonhuman* and *inhuman*

. . . .

. . . .

EXERCISE 1E

Write out, in the spaces provided, the words from Word List 1 for which a definition, synonym, or antonym is given on the next page. (Explanations of these terms are given in the Introduction.) When you are asked to give a root or a prefix, you should refer back to the preceding exercise; the information you require will be found there. Make sure that each of your answers has the same number of letters as there are spaces.

If all the words are filled in correctly, the boxes running down the answer spaces will give the first two words of a quotation from an ancient Greek writer named Diogenes Laertius, who lived from about 412 B.C. to 323 B.C. The quotation will be continued in Exercise 2E.

1. expressions of approval; applause

2. to translate from code into ordinary
   language
3. a synonym for *cower*

4. incapable of being explained

5. a fixed, mechanical way of learning
   or doing
6. an antonym for *bold*

7. a particular region or area

8. a region on the opposite side of the world

9. blurred and indistinct

10. a gathering of famous or brilliant people

11. a group or part considered superior

12. personal equipment or belongings

13. an antonym for *uplifting*

14. to call for particularly

15. occurring after death

16. a result or consequence, often
    unpleasant
17. to speak in protest; to object

WORDLY WISE 1

ANTIPODES may be used with the singular or plural form of the verb (the *antipodes* is located. . . . the *antipodes* are found. . . .). When referring to a specific place, such as Australia and New Zealand, the word is generally capitalized (a journey from England to the *Antipodes*).

A GALAXY is a vast number of stars making up a group or system occurring anywhere in the universe. When we speak of the Galaxy (with a capital *g*), we refer to the Milky Way, the galaxy of which our sun and its planets are a part.

PLAUDIT is nearly always used in the plural (the *plaudits* of the crowd).

AQUEDUCT	ELICIT	INTERROGATE
CARAVAN	EXHILARATING	PRIMITIVE
CHASTISE	FARRIER	PUGNACIOUS
DEMEAN	GENIUS	RANK
EDIFYING	GIRD	WEND
	INTER	

Look up the words above in your dictionary. Note that some of the words have more than one meaning. When you feel that you know *all* the meanings of *all* the words, go on to the exercise below.

EXERCISE 2A

From the four choices under each phrase or sentence, you are to mark the one that is closest in meaning to the word appearing in italics. When the same word appears more than once, you should note that it is being used in a different sense.

1. a woman of *genius*
(a) supernatural powers (b) great mental abilities (c) great physical strength (d) undeniable good looks

2. to build an *aqueduct*
(a) boat that planes over water (b) structure for conveying water (c) tunnel through a mountain (d) artificial fountain or waterfall

3. a *pugnacious* person
(a) foolishly naive (b) quarrelsomely aggressive (c) quietly confident (d) extremely mild-mannered

4. He is a *farrier*.
(a) one who keeps pigs (b) one who trains racehorses (c) one who shoes horses (d) one who deals in furs

5. a desert *caravan*
(a) group of travelers (b) watering place (c) clump of cacti (d) tribe of early people

6. a circus *caravan*
(a) troupe of performers (b) large canvas tent (c) large covered wagon (d) sawdust ring

7. an *exhilarating* experience
(a) frightening (b) depressing (c) invigorating (d) shocking

8. to *wend* slowly
(a) travel (b) rotate (c) rise (d) fall

9. *girded* by trees
(a) sparsely covered (b) encircled (c) crisscrossed (d) thickly covered

10. He *girded* on his sword.
(a) raised in salute (b) fastened with a belt (c) replaced in its scabbard (d) raised in battle

11. to *inter* a body
(a) bury (b) dig up (c) examine (d) preserve

12. *rank* weeds
(a) slender (b) coarse (c) edible (d) gone to seed

13. in *ranks*
(a) circles (b) great numbers (c) rows (d) small groups

14. *rank* fish
(a) freshwater (b) strong-smelling (c) raw (d) dried

15. to *rank* them
(a) make fun of (b) arrange in order (c) replace (d) defeat with ease

16. a *rank* injustice
(a) unintended (b) trivial (c) universal (d) extreme

17. to *chastise* someone
    (a) punish (b) warn (c) fear (d) reward

18. to *interrogate* someone
    (a) abandon (b) question (c) terrify (d) replace

19. to *elicit* a reply
    (a) demand (b) question (c) call forth (d) compose

20. *primitive* methods
    (a) effective (b) crude (c) uncertain (d) complicated

21. the *primitive* church
    (a) universal (b) earliest (c) modern (d) reformed

22. Don't *demean* yourself.
    (a) excuse (b) degrade (c) underestimate (d) deceive

23. an *edifying* experience
    (a) frightening (b) pleasant (c) instructive (d) boring

Check your answers against the correct ones below. The answers are not in order; this is to prevent your eye from catching sight of the correct ones before you have had a chance to do the exercise on your own.

4c. 13c. 16d. 21b. 18b. 11a. 1b. 15b. 6c. 12b. 23c. 19c. 3b. 7c. 20b. 5a. 14b. 22b. 9b. 8a. 10b. 2b. 17a.

Go back to your dictionary and look up again those words for which you gave incorrect answers. Only after doing this should you go on to the next exercise.

EXERCISE 2B

Each word in Word List 2 is used four times in the sentences below; one of the sentences in each group uses the word incorrectly. You are to circle the letter that precedes that sentence. Do not circle more than one letter in any one group.

1. (a) His *pugnacious* manner made the smaller children afraid of him. (b) Her *pugnacity* showed itself whenever she was refused what she wanted. (c) These explosive shells are *pugnacious* enough to pierce six-inch steel plates. (d) Bush pigs are naturally *pugnacious* and will put up a successful fight against a leopard.

2. (a) The car was *exhilarating* down the hill at an ever increasing speed. (b) The air in the mountains is quite *exhilarating*. (c) She was *exhilarated* by the news that she had been accepted by the college of her choice. (d) Her first trip in an airplane proved to be a most *exhilarating* experience.

3. (a) "The evil that men do lives after them, The good is oft *interred* with their bones"—Shakespeare. (b) She did not permit our warnings to *inter* her from going ahead with her plans. (c) The *interment* took place yesterday in the West Village Cemetery. (d) The body was *interred* in the little graveyard on the hill.

4. (a) Any student who interrupted another student was *chastised*. (b) I was *chastised* to discover that I had locked the car with keys inside it. (c) The *chastisement* of a child should always be carried out in a humane way. (d) She kept a cane on top of the cupboard and *chastised* the children with it whenever necessary.

5. (a) The *primitive* church is the name given to the Christian church as it existed up to about A.D. 300. (b) A child's *primitive* teeth are replaced by permanent teeth after a few years. (c) The first horseless carriages were *primitive* affairs compared to the modern automobile.

(d) *Primitive* people first learned to use tools during the Stone Age.

6. (a) Horses, donkeys, and zebras belong to the same *genius*. (b) That boy seems to have a *genius* for getting into trouble. (c) These instructions are so complicated that it would take a *genius* to figure them out. (d) Leonardo da Vinci—painter, sculptor, architect, engineer, and inventor—was one of the greatest *geniuses* ever known.

7. (a) In the days before the automobile replaced the horse, every village had its *farrier*. (b) It was the groom's job to feed and *farrier* the horses. (c) A *farrier's* knife had a curved blade for trimming the horse's hoof before shoeing. (d) Although not a qualified veterinarian, the *farrier* was often called upon to treat sick horses.

8. (a) The river quietly *wends* its way across field and woodland. (b) The young men left the inn and *wended* their way home. (c) As her fever grew worse, her mind began to *wend*. (d) "Through the fields and the woods and over the walls I have *wended*"—Robert Frost.

9. (a) All *ranks* from captain on down are expected to attend the meeting. (b) "O, my offense is *rank*," cries Claudius in Shakespeare's **Hamlet**. (c) South Africa *ranks* first among the diamond producing nations. (d) The garden had been neglected for years, and coarse *ranks* grew everywhere.

10. The police conducted an intensive *interrogation* of all the suspects in the case. (b) He acted as *interrogator* when the captured soldiers were questioned. (c) We may have to *interrogate* everyone in the house to find the culprit. (d) If the president dies, the office automatically *interrogates* to the vice-president.

11. (a) She claims that appearing in television commercials *demeans* the status of actors. (b) The librarian said the story was *demeaning* to women. (c) You *demean* yourself by telling these petty lies. (d) She spoke a strange language, and none of us could *demean* what she was saying.

12. (a) The water is *aqueducted* here through these large pipes. (b) The *aqueducts* built by the Romans were so well constructed that many of them are still standing. (c) *Aqueducts* were built with a slight slope so that the water would flow gently downhill. (d) To transport the water across the valley, an *aqueduct* several hundred feet high was built.

13. (a) A number of merchants left the *caravan* when it reached the oasis. (b) The three *caravans* of Christopher Columbus were named the **Niña**, the **Pinta**, and the **Santa María**. (c) The large, brightly-painted *caravans* of the circus filled the children with excitement. (d) The *caravan* was attacked several times by bandits as it crossed the desert.

14. (a) He *girded* on his sword and gave the signal to begin the battle. (b) A red sash was *girded* around her waist. (c) We must *gird* ourselves for a prolonged and bitter fight. (d) With a mighty leap the horse *girded* the river.

15. (a) He failed to *elicit* any support from those he approached. (b) Her question *elicited* only blank stares from the class. (c) He was engaged in smuggling and other *elicit* activities. (d) Her remarks *elicited* much laughter from the audience.

16. (a) She claimed that her stay at the college had been a most *edifying* experience. (b) The old schoolmaster's task was to *edify* the young people placed in his care. (c) The galleries and museums of our city are for the *edification* of all. (d) I suspected that she was *edifying* the facts of the case to show herself in as favorable a light as possible.

EXERCISE 2C

Rewrite each of the sentences below, replacing the italicized word or phrase with a word from Word List 2 and writing the word in the form that fits the rest of the sentence. Use each word only once. Write your answers in the spaces provided.

1. The engineer who designed this *structure used for conveying water* must have been a *person of great creative ability*.

   . . . .

   . . . .

2. The *person who shoes horses* is extremely *quarrelsome and aggressive*.

   . . . .

   . . . .

3. My most *exciting and invigorating* experience was accompanying a *group of travelers crossing the desert* in Libya.

   . . . .

   . . . .

4. After the body has been *put into the grave*, the mourners will *slowly make* their way back to the church.

   . . . .

   . . . .

5. The lake was *encircled* by clumps of *thick, coarse* weeds.

   . . . .

   . . . .

6. The children were *severely punished* for being so unkind to the new student.

   . . . .

   . . . .

7. The prisoner did not object to being *questioned closely*, but our efforts *brought forth* no information that was useful to us.

   . . . .

   . . . .

8. Your talk was most *instructive and morally uplifting* as well as being quite enjoyable.

   . . . .

   . . . .

9. The living quarters he offered me were so *crude and lacking in refinement* that I refused to *degrade* myself by accepting his offer to stay.

   . . . .

   . . . .

10

The Latin root *primus* (first) occurs in a number of English words and in some foreign phrases which have come into the English language. PRIMITIVE is based on this root and means "of the earliest times; first." Its secondary meaning, "crude; lacking refinement or sophistication," comes from the same root because the first versions of something often lack the refinement of later developments.

Give brief definitions of the following words and phrases, each of which is based on the Latin *primus*.

1. *prima donna*

   . . . .

   . . . .

2. *primary color*

   . . . .

   . . . .

3. *prime minister*

   . . . .

   . . . .

4. *primer*

   . . . .

   . . . .

5. *prima facie*

   . . . .

   . . . .

6. *prime meridian*

   . . . .

   . . . .

EXERCISE 2E

Write out, in the spaces provided, the words from Word List 2 for which a definition, synonym, or antonym is given on the next page. When you are asked to give a root or a prefix, you should refer back to the preceding exercise; the information you require will be found there. Make sure that each of your answers has the same number of letters as there are spaces. A definition followed by a number is a review word; the number gives the Word List from which it is taken.

If all the words are filled in correctly, the boxes running down the answer spaces will continue the quotation begun earlier.

1. a structure used for conveying water

2. an antonym for *moron*

3. to put into a grave

4. to lower in esteem

5. a fixed, mechanical way of learning (1)

6. to make one's way leisurely

7. quarrelsome; aggressive

8. to draw out; to bring forth

9. to punish, especially by beating

10. to question thoroughly

11. a Latin root meaning "first"

12. an antonym for *sophisticated*

13. one who shoes horses

14. morally improving or instructing

15. strong smelling

16. a synonym for *encircle*

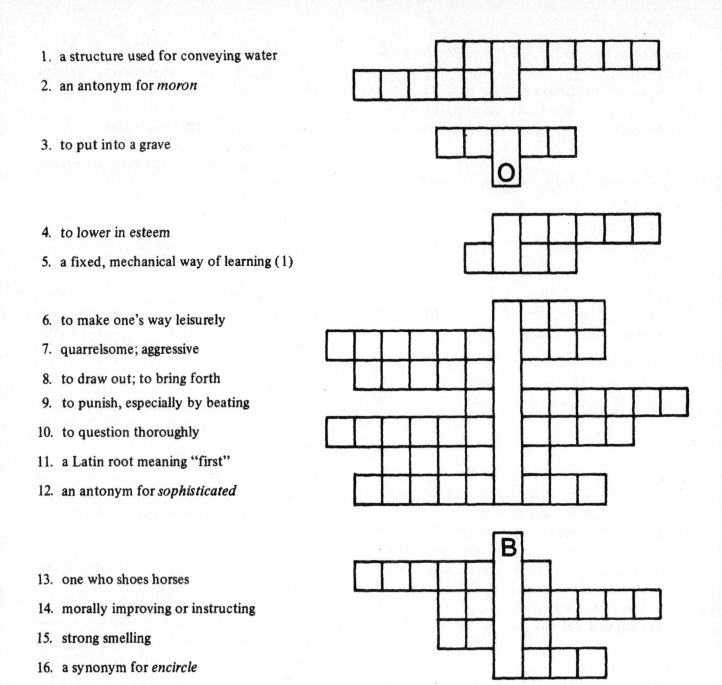

WORDLY WISE 2

A CARAVAN usually refers to a group of travelers crossing the desert on camels; such travelers would spend each night at a *caravansary*, a sort of desert inn. Because of its romantic associations with the desert, this word is sometimes used poetically to refer to an inn or stopping place of any kind.

DEMEAN originally meant "to conduct oneself." (She *demeaned* herself like a lady.) It still retains this meaning although it is not commonly used today. The current meaning, "to lower in esteem" (It is *demeaning* to lie to protect oneself), is considered incorrect by those who believe words should have fixed and unchanging meanings. However, this is an example of how words pass into and out of usage to meet particular needs and not to conform to any one person's view of what is correct and incorrect. See also *demeanor* (Word List 11).

In addition to meaning "to encircle," and "to fasten as with a belt," the verb GIRD also means "to prepare (oneself) for a struggle or a test of strength." (The students *girded* themselves for a difficult exam.)

Note that INTER, in addition to meaning "to place in a grave," is a prefix meaning "between" (to *inter*cept a pass is to seize the ball between the passer and the receiver).

Word List 3

AEGIS	ENGRAVE	LUCRE
BUDGET	EWER	ODOROUS
CARIES	FABULOUS	RARITY
CHRONICLE	GIG	SINISTER
DEEM	HISTORIC	TRIAD
DIALOGUE	HYPOTHETICAL	

Look up the words above in your dictionary. Note that some of the words have more than one meaning. When you feel that you know *all* the meanings of *all* the words, go on to the exercise below.

EXERCISE 3A

From the four choices under each phrase or sentence, you are to mark the one that is closest in meaning to the word appearing in italics. When the same word appears more than once, you should note that it is being used in a different sense.

1. a design *engraved* in metal
   (a) covered (b) cut (c) cast (d) copied

2. an *odorous* place
   (a) forbidden (b) of bad reputation (c) pleasantly-situated (d) sweet-smelling

3. a *triad* of symptoms
   (a) group of three (b) group of four (c) group of five (d) group of seven

4. a *sinister* plan
   (a) simple (b) practical (c) complicated (d) evil

5. to fill the *ewer*
   (a) ice bucket (b) water pitcher (c) leather bottle (d) wooden trough

6. the *dialogue* in a play
   (a) main idea (b) conversation (c) high point (d) list of characters

7. a *dialogue* between the two churches
   (a) holy war (b) continuous exchange of views (c) running feud (d) offer of mutual assistance

8. the captain's *gig*
   (a) tour of duty (b) small ship's boat (c) private quarters (d) badge of rank

9. to arrive in a *gig*
   (a) one-horse sleigh (b) two-wheeled carriage (c) single-engined plane (d) two-passenger canoe

10. to *gig* fish
    (a) cook on a spit (b) hook through the body (c) remove the scales from (d) catch in large nets

11. suffering from *caries*
    (a) an infection of the skin (b) poor eyesight (c) loss of hearing (d) tooth decay

12. *fabulous* adventures
    (a) highly dangerous (b) in foreign lands (c) almost incredible (d) of long ago

13. much *lucre*
    (a) good fortune (b) money (c) suffering (d) joy

14. the *rarity* of the air
    (a) sweet smell (b) lack of density (c) degree of moisture (d) lack of motion

15. That is a *rarity*.
    (a) obviously false statement (b) object valued because of its scarcity (c) obviously fake work of art (d) piece of incredibly good fortune

16. to *deem* it so
    (a) fear (b) believe (c) love (d) underrate

17. to *budget* one's energy
(a) waste (b) use carefully (c) begrudge
(d) measure precisely

18. a revised *budget*
(a) plan of income and expenses (b) plan of attack (c) estimate of total cost (d) estimate of needed repairs

19. under the *aegis* of the U.N.
(a) international law (b) dome (c) sponsorship (d) roof

20. an *historic* document
(a) long-forgotten (b) of the ancient world (c) important in history (d) in the original handwriting

21. an exciting *chronicle*
(a) journey to a foreign land (b) discovery of great importance (c) record of historical events (d) passage in a symphony

22. a *hypothetical* situation
(a) that could quickly become dangerous
(b) supposed for the sake of argument
(c) found in fiction but not in real life
(d) that keeps repeating itself

Check your answers against the correct ones below. The answers are not in order; this is to prevent your eye from catching sight of the correct ones before you have had a chance to do the exercise on your own.

8b. 3a. 14b. 17b. 21c. 15b. 13b. 2d. 11d. 6b. 19c. 20c. 5b. 22b. 4d. 1b. 12c. 10b. 18a. 16b. 9b. 7b.

Go back to your dictionary and look up again those words for which you gave incorrect answers. Only after doing this should you go on to the next exercise.

EXERCISE 3B

Each word in Word List 3 is used four times in the following sentences; one of the sentences in each group uses the word incorrectly. You are to circle the letter that precedes that sentence. Do not circle more than one letter in any one group.

1. (a) She became extremely *hypothetical* and had to be given a sedative. (b) Consider the *hypothetical* case of a man forced to choose between saving his wife or his mother. (c) The theory that sunspots affect the weather is merely an *hypothesis*. (d) The book uses a number of *hypothetical* cases to illustrate its various points.

2. (a) She completed her Ph. D. under the *aegis* of the physics department chair. (b) The lecturer is giving the talk under the *aegis* of the local university. (c) A large tarpaulin can be used as an *aegis* to protect the car. (d) The unfailing *aegis* of the law protects the weak and the strong alike.

3. (a) The *rarity* of the air at this height makes breathing difficult. (b) The *rarity* of the actor's appearances made them all the more appreciated. (c) An opera star who can both sing and act is indeed a *rarity*. (d) The *rarity* of the prisoner's condition was due to his inadequate diet.

4. (a) The dentist found only two *caries* when she examined my teeth yesterday. (b) The addition of fluorides to water supplies reduces the incidence of dental *caries* in the population. (c) Dental *caries* is treated by a dentist. (d) Too much sugar in the diet is a major cause of *caries*.

5. (a) A *ewer* usually gives birth to two lambs in the spring. (b) I poured the water from the *ewer* into the bowl and washed my hands and face. (c) I apologized for breaking off the handle of the *ewer*. (d) On the washstand was a bowl and *ewer* filled with water.

6. (a) That was an *odorous* trick you played on him. (b) The room was made pleasantly *odorous* by the basket of fruit on the dining room table. (c) I well remember the hot, *odorous* bread, pulled fresh from the oven. (d) She lay back peacefully, inhaling the *odorous* air of the orchard.

7. (a) She suffers from a *chronicle* form of the disease, and there is little that her doctors can do for her. (b) The Anglo-Saxon *Chronicle* is an historical account of life in England during the years A.D. 900 to 1200. (c) A number of novelists have *chronicled* the rise to power of the French middle class. (d) A *chronicle* play deals with a theme from history and consists of a number of loosely connected scenes.

8. (a) Because we were overspending, we decided to draw up a weekly *budget*. (b) In her will, the mother *budgeted* her fortune equally between her two children. (c) She has so many demands made on her that she must *budget* her time carefully. (d) The software company's *budget* exceeds the million dollar mark.

9. (a) How could they betray their country for mere *lucre*? (b) The enemy demanded five thousand gold *lucres* for the return of the king's son. (c) There is more to life than simply amassing *lucre* to hand on to one's children. (d) She disapproved of her friend's gambling and referred to the winnings as "filthy *lucre*."

10. (a) One *gigs* for fish by dragging an assortment of hooks through the water. (b) The *gig*, drawn by a single horse, was a popular mode of transportation in the days before the automobile. (c) The entire crew stood at attention as the captain stepped from the *gig* and boarded the ship. (d) We danced a merry *gig* to the lively sound of the fiddle.

11. (a) His *sinister* smile caused us to shiver with fear. (b) A *sinister* plot to kill the queen and put her brother on the throne was discovered just in time. (c) He *sinistered* up to me and said something out of the side of his mouth. (d) *Sinister* black clouds piled up on the horizon, threatening a violent storm.

12. (a) An *engraved* invitation is one printed from an etched or carved plate. (b) The events of that night are deeply *engraved* on his memory. (c) The bullet *engraved* a terrible wound in the woman's leg. (d) An *engraving* is a design or picture printed from an etched or carved plate.

13. (a) The *historic* voyage of Christopher Columbus is celebrated every October 12th. (b) She has written a couple of dozen *historic* novels dealing mostly with colonial times. (c) The Declaration of Independence is truly an *historic* document. (d) We spent a day touring the *historic* battlefield at Gettysburg.

14. (a) Take whatever steps you *deem* necessary. (b) He *deems* himself a liberal, but his actions indicate otherwise. (c) It is *deemed* advisable to remain silent in this matter. (d) She stared into space, *deeming* quietly to herself.

15. (a) The story she told was obviously *fabulous*, and no one believed it. (b) The *fabulous* wealth of the Incas enriched the coffers of Spain. (c) She told the story of the *fabulous* German tailor who made feather clothes for people who wanted to fly. (d) The *fabulous* adventures of Sinbad the Sailor have enthralled generations of children.

16. (a) Many of Plato's works are written in the form of *dialogues* between Socrates and his fellow Athenians. (b) A person speaking a New England *dialogue* might not be understood in the South. (c) The playwright is skillful at writing *dialogue* that sounds natural and convincing. (d) Pope John was instrumental in initiating the present *dialogue* between the Catholic and Protestant churches.

17. (a) The flu patients show the usual *triad* of symptoms: watery eyes, runny noses, aching muscles. (b) King Neptune is usually shown holding a *triad*, or three-pronged spear. (c) The painting was of the Fates, that formidable *triad* of goddesses who controlled the span of human life. (d) On her desk was a statue of that famous *triad*, the monkeys who see no evil, hear no evil, and speak no evil.

Rewrite each of the sentences below, replacing the italicized word or phrase with a word from Word List 3 and writing the word in the form that fits the rest of the sentence. Use each word only once. Write your answers in the spaces provided.

1. It is because it begins the *record of historical events* of our nation that Columbus's voyage is *considered* so *important in our history*.

   . . . .

   . . . .

2. A painting of this famous *group of three* is *an object prized because of its scarceness*.

   . . . .

   . . . .

3. The group has a very large *sum of money allotted for its use* and operates under the *protection and sponsorship* of the state governor.

   . . . .

   . . . .

4. Driven by dreams of *riches* thousands of people headed for the *almost incredibly* rich goldfields of the Klondike.

   . . . .

   . . . .

5. The garden of the old house was *fragrant* with summer blossoms, and there seemed nothing *suggestive of evil* about it in the daytime.

   . . . .

6. The *conversation that takes place in the story* between the two passengers in the *two-wheeled, horse-drawn carriage* is richly comic.

   . . . .

   . . . .

7. The *large, wide-mouthed water jug* rested in a silver bowl with a simple design *cut into the surface* around the rim.

   . . . .

   . . . .

8. The statement that *tooth decay* is caused by certain salts is merely *supposed to be true for the sake of the argument*.

   . . . .

   . . . .

universe	decimate
monotony	bicycle
demigod	quadrangle
pentagon	octopus
kilometer	quintuplet
hemisphere	millipede

You will recall that the word TRIAD is derived from the Greek root *tri* (three). In a dictionary that gives word origins, look up the words listed above. Basing your answers on the Greek and Latin roots of these words, complete the sentences below by filling in the blank spaces.

1. October was the . . . . month of the Roman calendar.

2. *Mono* is a . . . . root and means . . . .

3. Biweekly payments are made every . . . . weeks.

4. To quadruple something is to increase it . . . . .fold.

5. *Hemi* is a . . . . root and means . . . .

6. The word *decade* is derived from the . . . . root meaning . . . .

7. A pentagram is a . . . . -pointed star.

8. The word *union* is derived from the .root meaning . . . .

9. There are . . . . grams in a kilo-gram.

10. The word *quintet* is derived from the . . . . .root meaning . . . .

11. *Demi* is a . . . . root and means . . . .

12. There are . . . . millimeters in a meter.

EXERCISE 3E

Write out, in the spaces provided, the words from Word List 3 for which a definition, synonym, or antonym is given below. When you are asked to give a root or a prefix, you should refer back to the preceding exercise; the information you require will be found there. Make sure that each of your answers has the same number of letters as there are spaces. A definition followed by a number is a review word; the number gives the Word List from which it is taken.

If all the words are filled in correctly, the boxes running down the answer spaces will continue the quotation begun earlier.

1. bone or tooth decay

2. conversation in a play or story

3. a synonym for *consider*

4. a result or consequence, often unpleasant (1)

5. a large, covered wagon (2)

6. a record of historical events

7. a synonym for *fragrant*

8. riches; wealth

9. a plan adjusting income to expenditure

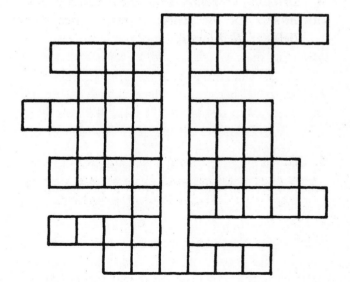

10. a large, wide-mouthed water pitcher

11. a Greek root meaning "half"

12. exciting and invigorating (2)

13. something prized because of its scarcity

14. barely credible; hard to believe

15. suggestive of harm or evil

16. an antonym for *actual*

17. support; protection

18. to cut or etch (a design or letters) in stone, metal, or wood
19. important in history

WORDLY WISE 3

AEGIS means "sponsorship; protection" (under the *aegis* of the federal government). It is a Greek word and was the name given to the shield of Zeus, chief of the gods of Mount Olympus. A sponsoring organization, therefore, presumably acts as a shield to protect those under its aegis.

DIALOGUE is sometimes spelled *dialog*; both spellings are correct.

FABULOUS originally meant "told about in fables," and hence that which is incredible or beyond reality. It is too frequently used as a synonym for "excellent" (a fabulous dancer); avoid this use.

HISTORIC means "important in history"; *historical* means "dealing with events of history." Harriet Beecher Stowe's *Uncle Tom's Cabin* is an *historic* novel because it helped change the course of history; Margaret Mitchell's *Gone With the Wind* is an *historical* novel because it deals with events in the history of our country.

The meanings of the following words are sometimes confused. ODOROUS means "giving off a (usually pleasant) odor." *Odoriferous* (from the Latin *odor*, "a smell," and the Latin *ferre*, "to bear") has the same meaning. This word and *odorous* are synonyms. *Malodorous* means "giving off an unpleasant smell"; this word and *odorous* are antonyms. *Odious* has nothing to do with smell; it comes from the Latin *odium* (hatred) and means "disgusting; offensive" (an odious lie).

You have now studied and worked with a total of fifty-one vocabulary words in this first chapter. The next exercise will give you a chance to use all these words. The crossword puzzle which follows has fifty-one clues; each clue is a definition of a word you have studied. Use each word from Word Lists 1, 2, and 3 only once and, unless otherwise stated, always in the form in which it appears in the Word List.

Each chapter in this book will end with a crossword puzzle, and each puzzle uses all the words from the three Word Lists in that chapter plus five to ten review words from earlier chapters for each puzzle after the first. You can spot the review words easily because their clues are followed by numbers; these numbers refer to the Word Lists from which the review words are taken.

ACROSS

1. crude; lacking refinement
5. to figure out the meaning of
8. money (used derogatively); riches
11. to state definitely
13. one who shoes horses
14. to lower in esteem; to degrade
15. supposed for the sake of argument
16. a person with great mental ability
17. unclear; lacking distinctness
19. to arrange in order
21. bone or tooth decay
24. not bold or forward; modest
26. sweet smelling; fragrant
28. an expression of approval
30. to schedule or plan carefully
34. morally uplifting or instructing
36. a record of historical events
38. threatening harm or evil
39. a mechanical way of learning
41. exciting and invigorating
43. lowering in esteem or self-respect
45. quarrelsome and aggressive
46. to punish, especially by beating
47. to make a deep impression on
48. to consider; to believe

DOWN

1. occurring after death
2. incapable of being explained
3. to draw out; to bring forth
4. to make one's way; to travel
6. personal equipment or belongings
7. something valued because it is scarce
9. a group of travelers, especially one crossing the desert
10. to speak in protest; to object
12. to put into a grave; to bury
13. hard to believe; incredible
16. to encircle or fasten, as with a belt
18. a particular region or area
20. a structure used for conveying water
23. a large, wide-mouthed water jug
25. to question thoroughly
27. to draw back in fear
29. the region on the opposite side of the world
31. a vast number of stars taken as a group
32. a result or consequence, usually unpleasant
33. important in history
35. an exchange of views between two persons or two groups
37. protection; sponsorship
40. a group considered superior
42. a group of three closely related persons or things
44. a small ship's boat

Chapter Two

Word List 4

ABET	INCORRIGIBLE	REPUDIATE
ACCORD	INSIGHT	REVERENT
AWL	MOCCASIN	SAGE
COERCE	OUST	TEXTILE
CONTRITE	PESTILENCE	UMBRAGE
FODDER		

Look up the words above in your dictionary. Note that some of the words have more than one meaning. When you feel that you know *all* the meanings of *all* the words, go on to the exercise below.

EXERCISE 4A

From the four choices under each phrase or sentence, you are to mark the one that is closest in meaning to the word appearing in italics. When the same word appears more than once, you should note that it is being used in a different sense.

1. a *reverent* attitude
   (a) happily carefree (b) deliberately offensive (c) solemnly respectful (d) inappropriately flippant

2. to use an *awl*
   (a) ax used for dressing wood (b) iron block on which metal is hammered (c) small, two-edged surgeon's knife (d) small pointed tool used for making holes

3. a *sage* reply
   (a) foolish (b) wise (c) unclear (d) mocking

4. to use *sage*
   (a) great care (b) a beef extract (c) good judgment (d) an odorous seasoning

5. He is a *sage*.
   (a) very old man (b) man who drinks to excess (c) very wise man (d) man who eats to excess

6. a *contrite* manner
   (a) remorseful (b) arrogant (c) polite (d) gentle

7. a pair of *moccasins*
   (a) Eskimo snowshoes (b) buckskin trousers (c) antique dueling pistols (d) heelless leather shoes

8. a water *moccasin*
   (a) floating plant (b) poisonous snake (c) air-breathing fish (d) gnatlike insect

9. He is *incorrigible*.
   (a) incapable of being reformed (b) suffering from a fatal disease (c) never satisfied (d) confused

10. a clear *insight*
    (a) explanation of something (b) understanding of something (c) example of something (d) conscience

11. to *repudiate* a statement
    (a) have published (b) refuse to accept (c) make a reply to (d) draw up

12. to *abet* wrongdoing
    (a) report (b) encourage (c) cover up (d) put a stop to

13. to *oust* someone
    (a) envy (b) expel (c) mock (d) injure

14. to take *umbrage*
    (a) retaliate (b) feel offended (c) steal (d) feel overjoyed

15. lots of *fodder*
    (a) stuffing for pillows (b) fiber used for insulation (c) wool clipped from sheep (d) coarse animal feed

16. to fear the *pestilence*
(a) widespread shortage of food (b) disease that rages unchecked (c) floods spreading over a wide area (d) fire that rages unchecked

17. to *coerce* someone
(a) persuade by making promises to (b) attempt to imitate (c) compel by making threats against (d) raise the standards of

18. to *accord* an honor
(a) refuse (b) award (c) appreciate (d) accept

19. in *accord*
(a) doubt (b) agreement (c) dispute (d) disgrace

20. of one's own *accord*
(a) social group (b) better nature (c) judgment (d) free will

21. to produce *textiles*
(a) pure metal bars (b) woven fabrics (c) processed foods (d) articles of furniture

Check your answers against the correct ones below. The answers are not in order; this is to prevent your eye from catching sight of the correct ones before you have had a chance to do the exercise on your own.

17c. 3b. 7d. 6a. 12b. 19b. 2d. 20d. 11b. 1c. 15d. 10b. 5c. 16b. 21b. 18b. 8b. 14b. 4d. 13b. 9a.

Go back to your dictionary and look up again those words for which you gave incorrect answers. Only after doing this should you go on to the next exercise.

EXERCISE 4B

Each word in Word List 4 is used four times in the following sentences; one of the sentences in each group uses the word incorrectly. You are to circle the letter that precedes that sentence. Do not circle more than one letter in any one group.

1. (a) Threats of dismissal and other *coercive* measures were used to force the men to work harder. (b) She was *coerced* into helping the others. (c) A rat will turn and fight if *coerced* into a corner. (d) Persuasion is better than *coercion* in getting people to do what you want.

2. (a) You will give *umbrage* to them if you do not invite them. (b) He took *umbrage* at my remarks although I had not intended them to be critical. (c) "I resent that remark," he *umbraged*. (d) She is not a woman to take *umbrage* unless she has been given good cause.

3. (a) The basketball player *repudiated* her opponent's attempts to block her shots. (b) She *repudiated* many of the beliefs she had held as a child. (c) The new government *repudiated* all the debts incurred before it came to power. (d) She *repudiated* the statement that had been attributed to her.

4. (a) *Moccasins* were the usual footwear of many Native Americans. (b) The settlers planted *moccasin* seeds to ensure a supply of food for the winter. (c) The water *moccasin* is a poisonous snake found in the southeast United States. (d) A heeled shoe resembling the original *moccasin* is sold in most shoe stores.

5. (a) The story she told us is in *accord* with the known facts. (b) They *accorded* the two sets of figures and found that they matched perfectly. (c) Did he go with you of his own *accord*, or did you force him to go? (d) She was *accorded* many honors during her lifetime.

6. (a) The soldiers objected to being treated as mere cannon *fodder* and revolted against their officers. (b) His grandfather, an old *fodder* of ninety, was the life of the party. (c) The hay in the barn is used as *fodder* for the horses. (d) Gossips, misers, and busybodies have been *fodder* for comedians since the time of the ancient Greeks.

7. (a) He was aided and *abetted* in this crime by his older brother. (b) The general, *abetted* by his aides, made a series of bad blunders. (c) To *abet* someone in the execution of a crime is a serious offense. (d) Parents should *abet* their children to love books.

8. (a) He tried to bend the metal bar into shape, but it was too *incorrigible*. (b) She is an *incorrigible* liar, and I do not believe a word she says. (c) That prison houses the most *incorrigible* prisoners in the state. (d) I've tried to get her to change her ways, but she is quite *incorrigible*.

9. (a) I appreciated the *sage* advice she offered me. (b) She *saged* the problem carefully before offering an answer. (c) *Sage* is used to give flavor to sausages, poultry, and pork dishes. (d) His profound thought has helped people understand themselves better, and for this he is regarded as a *sage*.

10. (a) The *textile* industry in this country faces tough competition from imported cotton goods. (b) Raw cotton from the South is used in the manufacture of *textiles*. (c) She wore a brightly colored *textile* which she had bought in Mexico. (d) The new *textile*-producing machines threw many weavers out of work.

11. (a) The *pestilence* was spread by germ-ridden rats. (b) War, famine, and *pestilence* kept the population from becoming too large. (c) The doctor thought the woman was suffering from *pestilence* and ordered her to go to the hospital. (d) *Pestilent* diseases have been virtually wiped out in western countries.

12. (a) He was *ousted* from the presidency of the company. (b) Any persons who try to disrupt the meeting will be *ousted* by the ushers. (c) The doctor *ousted* a metal fragment that had been embedded in the man's arm. (d) The poodle has *ousted* the spaniel from its position as America's favorite dog.

13. (a) *Awls* have round, pointed blades, shaped and bent to suit different purposes. (b) The leather must be *awled* into the required shape before being sewn. (c) A bootmaker uses an *awl* to make holes in leather. (d) Mark the places to be drilled with the point of the *awl*.

14. Psychiatrists must have good *insight* into the minds of those they help. (b) The book shows extraordinary *insight* into the problems of today's city dweller. (c) She made a few *insightful* observations about the causes of the economy's improvement. (d) She was able to *insight* many things that the ordinary person would pass over.

15. (a) The judge urged the prisoner to have a *contrite* heart. (b) Their tear-stained faces were the evidence of *contrition* for telling a lie. (c) The children were very *contrite* after I scolded them for fighting. (d) She was forced to *contrite* the children when they received poor grades.

16. (a) The audience listened *reverently* to the world-famous pianist. (b) Saint Francis showed *reverence* for all living things. (c) The minister of this church is the *Reverent* Sarah Black. (d) He approached his favorite author and spoke to him in a *reverent* voice.

EXERCISE 4C

Rewrite each of the following sentences, replacing the italicized word or phrase with a word from Word List 4 and writing the word in the form that fits the rest of the sentence. Use each word only once. Write your answers in the spaces provided.

1. Did you *give help and encouragement to* her in her attempt to *remove* the new members?

....

....

2. His voice was *full of respect and awe* when he spoke to the *wise old man*.

. . . .

. . . .

3. To make these *flexible, heelless, leather shoes*, you will need a knife, needle and thread, and a *sharply-pointed hand tool for making holes*.

. . . .

. . . .

4. He is really quite *incapable of being reformed* although he pretends to be *full of remorse*.

. . . .

. . . .

5. Do not try to *use threats to compel* her into joining you, or she will take *offense*.

. . . .

. . . .

6. The doctors were in *general agreement* in regard to the causes of the *dreadful disease that continued to rage unchecked*.

. . . .

. . . .

7. Her great *ability to understand and to see* into the problem led her to *refuse to accept* such an easy solution.

. . . .

. . . .

8. The plant fibers are made into *woven fabrics*, and the leaves and roots are chopped up to make *coarse food for animals*.

. . . .

. . . .

EXERCISE 4D

The Anglo-Saxon prefix *a-* can mean variously "on," "in," "to," "of," or "at." It is found in such words as ABET (to lend aid *to*) and *aboard* (*on* a ship).

There is also a Greek prefix *a-* (also written *an-*) which means "without; lacking." It is found in such words as *anarchy* (*without* order) and *amorphous* (*without* definite shape).

Finally there is a Latin prefix *ab-* which may appear as *a-* or *abs-* and means "off," "from," or "away." To *avert* one's eyes is to turn them *away*; to *absolve* a person is to free him *from* blame.

Complete the words below by filling in the appropriate prefix from those above. In the parentheses state whether the prefix is Anglo-Saxon (A-S), Latin (L), or Greek (Gr). Check each word for spelling and accuracy. Give a brief definition of each word.

1. ____ MORAL   ( )

. . . .

. . . .

2. ____ TAIN   ( )

. . . .

. . . .

3. ____ DICATE   ( )

. . . .

. . . .

4. ____ BED   ( )

. . . .

5. ___ DUCT   (   )   8. ___ STERN   (   )

. . . .

. . . .

6. ___ THEIST   (   )   9. ___ USE   (   )

. . . .

. . . .

7. ___ KIN   (   )   10. ___ PATHY   (   )

. . . .

. . . .

EXERCISE 4E

Write out, in the spaces provided, the words from Word List 4 for which a definition, synonym, or antonym is given below. Make sure that each of your answers has the same number of letters as there are spaces. A definition followed by a number is a review word; the number gives the Word List from which it is taken.

If all the words are filled in correctly, the boxes running down the answer spaces will conclude the quotation begun in Exercise 1E.

1. an antonym for *acknowledge*

2. a synonym for *remorseful*

3. morally improving or instructive (2)

4. showing love, respect, or awe

5. a synonym for *agreement*

6. a feeling of being offended

24

7. coarse food for animals

8. to compel by making threats

9. a very wise man

10. incapable of being corrected or reformed

11. an antonym for *admit*

12. one who shoes horses (2)

13. to encourage or help, especially in wrongdoing

14. an understanding of the nature of something

15. a woven fabric or cloth

16. a disease that rages unchecked

17. a flexible, heelless, leather shoe

18. a pointed hand tool used for making holes

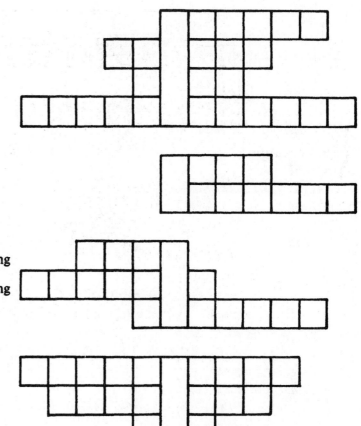

WORDLY WISE 4

In addition to its literal meaning, FODDER is used metaphorically in at least two ways. It can mean "human beings regarded for a certain purpose as an undifferentiated mass." (Soldiers sent to certain death in a war are referred to, somewhat bitterly, as "cannon fodder.") It can also mean "raw material for artistic creation."

Note that UMBRAGE, meaning "a feeling of being offended," is used only in the phrases "to take umbrage" and "to give umbrage."

Word List 5

AVERSE	REPUTABLE	TANGIBLE
CENSUS	ROISTERER	TOGA
DISCLAIM	SPAWN	TRANCE
EXTERMINATE	STIPULATE	VIGILANTE
HEMORRHAGE	SURPLUS	VINDICTIVE
INEXORABLE		

Look up the words above in your dictionary. Note that some of the words have more than one meaning. When you feel that you know *all* the meanings of *all* the words, go on to the following exercise.

EXERCISE 5A

From the four choices under each phrase or sentence, you are to mark the one that is closest in meaning to the word appearing in italics. When the same word appears more than once, you should note that it is being used in a different sense.

1. a *reputable* person
   (a) famous (b) respectable (c) intelligent
   (d) dishonest

2. *averse* to doing something
   (a) accustomed (b) unaccustomed (c) opposed (d) unopposed

3. to *exterminate* pests
   (a) guard against (b) destroy (c) put up with (d) control

4. in a *trance*
   (a) sleeplike state (b) fraction of a second (c) desperate situation (d) hurry

5. a small *surplus*
   (a) quantity short of what is needed (b) store of provisions (c) sum of money earning interest (d) quantity over what is needed

6. *tangible* evidence
   (a) that can be touched (b) easily disposed of (c) not allowable in court (d) based on what was heard or seen

7. *inexorable* progress
   (a) that proceeds in stages (b) that cannot be stopped (c) that brings blessings (d) that proceeds very slowly

8. a Roman *toga*
   (a) meeting of all citizens (b) loose outer garment (c) officer in the army (d) wild, drunken party

9. a *vindictive* person
   (a) revengeful (b) forgiving (c) intelligent (d) easily-deceived

10. She began to *hemorrhage*.
    (a) bleed heavily (b) grow sleepy (c) suffer great pain (d) improve slowly

11. to *spawn*
    (a) engage in quarrelsome disputes (b) produce young in large numbers (c) imitate what others have done (d) spy on one's neighbors

12. a *census* at regular intervals
    (a) election of local officials (b) official count of the population (c) plan for the country's economy (d) mass movement to another country

13. a band of *vigilantes*
    (a) people taking the law into their own hands (b) persons who pioneer in new territories (c) robbers who move from place to place (d) soldiers who spy on enemy positions

14. to *disclaim* responsibility
    (a) accept (b) determine (c) share (d) deny

15. a young *roisterer*
    (a) person learning a trade (b) person who sells from door to door (c) person celebrating noisily (d) person who joins a monastery

16. to *stipulate* certain conditions
    (a) get around (b) copy exactly (c) specify (d) observe

Check your answers against the correct ones below. The answers are not in order; this is to prevent your eye from catching sight of the correct ones before you have had a chance to do the exercise on your own.

6a. 11b. 16c. 4a. 1b. 12b. 3b. 15c. 13a. 9a. 8b. 10a. 2c. 7b. 5d. 14d.

Go back to your dictionary and look up again those words for which you gave incorrect answers. Only after doing this should you go on to the next exercise.

EXERCISE 5B

Each word in Word List 5 is used four times in the following sentences; one of the sentences in each group uses the word incorrectly. You are to circle the letter that precedes that sentence. Do not circle more than one letter in any one group.

1. (a) He *stipulated* in his will that his children were not to receive the money until they married. (b) We were *stipulated* from entering the building by two guards. (c) The house was left to the town with the *stipulation* that it always be open to the public. (d) She was careful to *stipulate* that payment would not be made until the work was done.

26

2. **(a)** If the money is still *disclaimed* after thirty days, it belongs to the finder. **(b)** He *disclaimed* all knowledge of the crime when the police questioned him. **(c)** The senator *disclaimed* the charge that she received money from certain oil interests. **(d)** Unless you issue a *disclaimer*, the public will believe these lies.

3. **(a)** The United States has conducted a *census* every ten years since 1790. **(b)** The *census* provides information on the social and economic conditions of the people. **(c)** The *census* reads all outgoing mail of soldiers fighting in critical areas. **(d)** Citizens are required by law to answer all questions on the *census*.

4. **(a)** Such childish behavior is *vindictive* of an immature mind. **(b)** The *vindictiveness* of his remarks shocked us all. **(c)** Such punishment is purely *vindictive* and is not intended to help the prisoners mend their ways. **(d)** He was a very *vindictive* man who never forgot an injury or an insult.

5. **(a)** She lay in a *trance*, her eyes staring sightlessly at the ceiling. **(b)** After swallowing the powder, he fell into a deep *trance*. **(c)** This drug induces a *trance*like state in the person who swallowed it. **(d)** The dogs were briefly *tranced* up with rope to prevent their escape.

6. **(a)** He has ruined his *reputation* by his misconduct. **(b)** The **New York Times** is a highly *reputable* newspaper. **(c)** She is *reputed* to be the richest woman in town. **(d)** She *disreputabled* herself at work by telling lies.

7. **(a)** The *roisterers* were arrested for creating a disturbance. **(b)** The students were known for their *roisterous* parties which lasted until dawn. **(c)** They love to go out with friends and *roister* until all hours. **(d)** There were seventy names on the *roister* of new members.

8. **(a)** She suffered a brain *hemorrhage* and was rushed to the hospital. **(b)** If the patient continues to *hemorrhage*, he will need a blood transfusion. **(c)** The doctor removed a large *hemorrhage* from the patient's lung. **(d)** Several severe *hemorrhages* had left her looking pale and exhausted.

9. **(a)** The disease continued its slow but *inexorable* course. **(b)** The glacier's *inexorable* advance continued along the northern border. **(c)** Oil deposits in the Middle East are almost *inexorable*. **(d)** We can make use of, but we cannot change the *inexorable* laws of the universe.

10. **(a)** It was *tangible* to everyone that the man was lying. **(b)** What is more subtle, more *intangible*, than the human soul! **(c)** Buildings and equipment are *tangible* assets. **(d)** She received their grateful thanks, but she had hoped for a more *tangible* reward.

11. **(a)** A large-scale nuclear war would *exterminate* all life on this earth. **(b)** The contract may be *exterminated* by either party on giving thirty days notice. **(c)** Within a few decades the Spaniards had *exterminated* the Carib Indians of Hispaniola. **(d)** This powder is used to *exterminate* household pests.

12. **(a)** Before the rule of law was established, justice in the Old West was often in the hands of *vigilantes*. **(b)** A band of *vigilantes* was organized to protect the town when law and order broke down. **(c)** The mother kept a *vigilante* eye on the sleeping baby. **(d)** The judge said he would take strong measures to end *vigilantism* in the territory.

13. **(a)** Some crime is *spawned* in the inner cities. **(b)** Salmon make their way up-river to *spawn*. **(c)** The spottail shiner is a freshwater fish that eats the *spawn* of other fish. **(d)** She *spawned* her watch to buy food for her family.

14. **(a)** Hundreds of Roman citizens attended the *toga* held every year in the emperor's palace.

(b) The *toga* was made of undyed woolen cloth and draped so as to leave the right arm free. (c) In this marbled hall togaed Roman senators once walked. (d) The dancers wore loose, colorful *togas* for their performance.

15. (a) The fifty dollar *surplus* of last year is cancelled by this year's fifty dollar deficit. (b) *Surplus* these various amounts and write down the total. (c) The sale of *surplus* wheat to Asian countries benefits everyone. (d) She covered the sofa with the material and used the *surplus* to make cushion covers.

16. (a) This dry spell is bound to have an *averse* effect on the crops. (b) She is *averse* to taking exercise. (c) He has a strong *aversion* to work. (d) He is not *averse* to a long walk in the evening.

EXERCISE 5C

Rewrite each of the sentences below, replacing the italicized word or phrase with a word from Word List 5 and writing the word in the form that fits the rest of the sentence. Use each word only once. Write your answers in the spaces provided.

1. The law *specifies* that an *official count of the population* be taken every ten years.

   . . . .

   . . . .

2. He *refuses to accept* any responsibility for errors, but he is not *unwilling to respond* to praise for his successes.

   . . . .

   . . . .

3. So *wicked and revengeful* was the queen that she determined to *destroy completely* all those who opposed her.

   . . . .

. . . .

4. The men he had thought were *merrymakers having a good time* were actually *members of a group banded together to take the law into their own hands.*

   . . . .

   . . . .

5. The salmon are caught as they swim upstream to *lay their eggs.*

   . . . .

   . . . .

6. If you have too much produce, sell the *amount that is above your needs* to a dealer you know is *trustworthy and has a good reputation.*

   . . . .

   . . . .

7. The ghost wore a *loose outer garment* draped around itself and stared ahead as though in a *deep, sleeplike state.*

   . . . .

   . . . .

8. The rising floodwaters were *relentless and incapable of being stopped.*

   . . . .

   . . . .

9. A supply of blood is kept available in case the patient begins to *bleed heavily.*

   . . . .

   . . . .

10. Hope, though not *capable of being touched or held physically*, is nevertheless real.

. . . .

. . . .

EXERCISE 5D

The Latin root *termin* means "boundary" and is found in such a word as EXTERMINATE. The Latin prefix *ex-* means "out."

Complete each of the words below, for which prefixes and suffixes have been supplied, by filling in the Latin root that means "boundary." Write out a brief definition of each word.

1. _____ US . . . .

. . . .

. . . .

2. IN_____ ABLE . . . .

. . . .

. . . .

3. _____ ATE . . . .

. . . .

4. INDE_____ ATE . . . .

. . . .

. . . .

5. _____ AL (adj.) . . . .

. . . .

. . . .

The prefix *ex-* is reduced to *e-* before the letters *b, d, g, l, m, n, r,* and *v*. Note that the prefix

ex- can mean "former," but when it is used this way, it is always set off by a hyphen (an ex-president).

Each of the words below is complete except for the prefix. Fill in the correct form of the Latin prefix that means "out," and give a brief definition of each word.

6. __MIGRATE . . . .

. . . .

. . . .

7. __RODE . . . .

. . . .

. . . .

8. __IT . . . .

. . . .

. . . .

9. __PEL . . . .

. . . .

. . . .

10. __RASE . . . .

. . . .

. . . .

EXERCISE 5E

Write out, in the spaces provided, the words from Word List 5 for which a definition, synonym, or antonym is given on the next page. When you are asked to give a root or a prefix, you should refer back to the preceding exercise; the information you require will be found there. Make sure that each of your answers has the same number of letters as there are spaces. A definition followed by a number is a review word; the number gives the Word List from which it is taken.

If all the words are filled in correctly, the boxes running down the answer spaces will give the first five words of a quotation from the writings of Edgar Watson Howe (1853-1937), American editor and writer on country life. Mr. Howe was known as "The Sage of Potato Hill."

The quotation will be continued in Exercise 6E.

1. of good reputation; respectable

2. not clear; uncertain (1)

3. unwilling; opposed

4. to destroy entirely; to wipe out

5. a Latin prefix meaning "out"

6. a Latin root meaning "boundary"

7. an antonym for *deficit*

8. an unnatural sleeplike state

9. a synonym for *relentless*

10. a loose outer garment, as worn in ancient Rome

11. an understanding of the nature of something (4)

12. spiteful and revengeful

13. one of a group taking the law into its own hands

14. a synonym for *touchable*

15. an official count of the population

16. to bleed heavily

17. to produce young in large numbers

18. one who celebrates noisily

19. an antonym for *admit*

20. to specify as a necessary condition

30

WORDLY WISE 5

Don't confuse AVERSE, which means "unwilling," with *adverse*, which means "hostile; unfriendly." (She was *averse* to going on the trip because of the *adverse* weather conditions.)

When SPAWN is used in connection with fish, oysters, and other aquatic animals, it means "to produce and deposit sex cells; to produce young." *Spawn* also can be a disparaging or contemptuous term when it refers to producing excessively or in large numbers. (Every year books are *spawned* by the millions.)

A VIGILANTE (with final "e," pronounced *vij-ǝ-LAN-ti*) is a member of a group formed to take the law into its own hands. *Vigilant* (pronounced *VIJ-ǝ-lǝnt*) is an adjective meaning "alert to danger; watchful." Note: the phonetic symbol ǝ indicates the vowel sound equivalent to *a* in *ago*; it is called a *schwa*.

Word List 6

ABSTRACT	DEMENTED	SIMILE
ADEPT	EARTHY	SLEAZY
ANTITHESIS	ECCENTRIC	SYNTHETIC
BETROTHED	REMIT	TEMPO
COPIOUS	SEPULCHER	UNDULATE
CREDULOUS		

Look up the words above in your dictionary. Note that some of the words have more than one meaning. When you feel that you know *all* the meanings of *all* the words, go on to the exercise below.

EXERCISE 6A

From the four choices under each phrase or sentence, you are to mark the one that is closest in meaning to the word appearing in italics. When the same word appears more than once, you should note that it is being used in a different sense.

1. a *copious* supply
   (a) plentiful (b) scarce (c) evenly distributed (d) variable

2. to *undulate* slowly
   (a) sink out of sight (b) swing in a circle (c) come into view (d) move in a wavelike manner

3. the *antithesis* of something
   (a) final result (b) chief cause (c) exact opposite (d) various parts

4. to increase the *tempo*
   (a) volume of activity (b) rate of activity (c) tax on imported goods (d) value of something

5. to *remit* the money
   (a) keep (b) send (c) account for (d) borrow

6. to *remit* sins
   (a) punish (b) ignore (c) commit (d) forgive

7. a *credulous* person
   (a) hard to convince (b) easily fooled (c) wasteful (d) extremely wealthy

8. *synthetic* fabrics
   (a) extremely delicate (b) composed of man-made fiber (c) hard wearing (d) costly

9. *earthy* humor
   (a) coarse (b) unintended (c) childish (d) cruel

10. an *adept* manner
    (a) sly (b) skillful (c) clumsy (d) polite

11. *abstract* ideas
    (a) acquired from books (b) absurdly impractical (c) dangerous (d) considered apart from any material object

12. to *abstract* certain passages
    (a) summarize (b) cross out (c) underline (d) memorize

13. an *abstract* explanation
    (a) concise (b) oversimplified (c) obviously false (d) difficult to understand

14. to be *abstracted*
    (a) easily deterred (b) absent-minded (c) easily annoyed (d) very knowledgeable

15. He is *demented*.
    (a) very easily led (b) mentally ill (c) very wise (d) ill-at-ease

16. a large *sepulcher*
    (a) church (b) tomb (c) sailing vessel (d) fortress

17. an example of a *simile*
    (a) a fourteen-line poem (b) directly expressed comparison between things (c) deliberately ambiguous statement (d) word stressed on each syllable

18 to visit one's *betrothed*
    (a) intended partner in a crime (b) intended partner in a business (c) intended partner in marriage (d) intended mother-in-law

19. an *eccentric* person
    (a) ill-tempered (b) oddly behaving (c) unhealthy (d) one-legged

20. *eccentric* wheels
    (a) turning in opposite directions (b) with axles not at their centers (c) of different sizes (d) having some fault

21. *sleazy* cloth
    (a) tightly woven (b) expensive (c) flimsy (d) man-made

22. a *sleazy* neighborhood
    (a) quiet (b) disreputable (c) friendly (d) wealthy

Check your answers against the correct ones below. The answers are not in order; this is to prevent your eye from catching sight of the correct ones before you have had a chance to do the exercise on your own.

17b. 3c. 7b. 6d. 12a. 19b. 2d. 20b. 11d. 1a. 22b. 15b. 10b. 5b. 16b. 21c. 18c. 8b. 14b. 4b. 13d. 9a.

Go back to your dictionary and look up again those words for which you gave incorrect answers.

Only after doing this should you go on the next exercise.

EXERCISE 6B

Each word in Word List 6 is used four times in the sentences below; one of the sentences in each group uses the word incorrectly. You are to circle the letter that precedes that sentence. Do not circle more than one letter in any one group.

1. (a) The marriage was *betrothed* by the parish priest in the little village church. (b) They were *betrothed* at the end of March and married a month later. (c) He gave a diamond pin to his *betrothed* on her birthday. (d) The *betrothal* of the two young people was an occasion for great rejoicing.

2. (a) This part of the hospital once housed patients who were *demented*. (b) She must be *demented* to carry on in such an outrageous manner. (c) The joyful screams from the fans of the winning team made them seem *demented*. (d) The court ordered that the sergeant be *demented* to the rank of private.

3. (a) The poem speaks of the wonderful *earthy* smell of a freshly dug garden. (b) He was a bluff, *earthy* man, and his home, though not elegant, was comfortable. (c) *Unearthy* screams came from the direction of the cellar. (d) Her *earthy* humor embarrassed some of the guests.

4. (a) Please *remit* the amount due by check or money order. (b) Do not *remit* to mention that it was my idea. (c) It is held that the power of the priest to *remit* sins is derived from God. (d) A *remittance* person was one who lived overseas and received regular sums of money from home.

5. (a) The pupil of the eye contracts in bright light and *undulates* in darkness. (b) The snake slipped into the bushes with a gentle *undulating* movement. (c) The dark waters of the harbor *undulated* and slapped against the sides of the boat. (d) The gently *undulating* hills stretched back as far as the eye could see.

6. (a) The dresses were made of some *sleazy* material that would not wear well. (b) The man was a *sleazy* character whose time was spent hanging around pool halls. (c) Her stomach felt slightly *sleazy* after the heavy meal. (d) At first glance her neighborhood looked *sleazy*, but it was really quite safe.

7. (a) There is a strong *simile* between Old English and German. (b) *Simile* and metaphor are the figurative language of poetry. (c) "As hard as a rock" is an example of a *simile*. (d) A *simile* is a figure of speech in which things of different categories are compared, often with an "as" or "like" construction.

8. (a) Her reasoning is too *abstract* for the average person to follow. (b) Justice is not an *abstract* idea, but something affecting the lives of all of us. (c) If we *abstract* three from five, how many remain? (d) She made an *abstract* of the senator's speech and circulated it among us.

9. (a) Cottons and woolens can be washed in this soap, but *synthetics* need special care. (b) The smiles of the welcoming committee seemed *synthetic*, and their words of greeting hollow. (c) His statement that I encouraged him in his wrongdoing is a *synthetic*. (d) *Synthetic* diamonds sell at much lower prices than real ones.

10. (a) The *tempo* of the campaign increased steadily as election day drew near. (b) The judge felt it was his duty to *tempo* justice with mercy. (c) The band plays at a very fast *tempo*. (d) The frenzied *tempo* of modern life is not to everyone's taste.

11. (a) The article was supplied with *copious* footnotes. (b) She wept *copiously* when she heard of her son's death. (c) We were feeling quite *copious* after the heavy meal. (d) *Copi-*

ous amounts of coffee and sandwiches were on hand.

12. (a) An *eccentric* triangle is one with all three angles different. (b) He was an *eccentric* and used to walk the streets handing out quarters. (c) His *eccentric* fashion sense made him stand out in a crowd. (d) An *eccentric* wheel has its axis located off center in order to convert rotary motion to a to-and-fro motion.

13. (a) The body was placed in the *sepulcher* and a large stone rolled over the opening. (b) The judge, in hollow *sepulchral* tones, sentenced the murderer to death. (c) They groped their way in the *sepulchral* darkness of the chamber. (d) She was treated with *sepulcher* for her cough.

14. (a) They are incapable of *adepting* themselves to changing conditions. (b) She is *adept* at analyzing personality traits from people's handwriting. (c) The playwright's *adeptness* at keeping the comedy moving briskly deserves our praise. (d) She is an *adept* at getting people to do what she wants.

15. (a) He must be extremely *credulous* to believe such an obviously false story. (b) Her statement that a flying saucer had landed was greeted with *incredulous* stares. (c) His story sounds *credulous*, but we must not make up our minds until we have all the facts. (d) His story strains *credulity* to the breaking point.

16. (a) Her attitude is the very *antithesis* of what I had been led to believe. (b) "Action, not words" is an example of *antithesis*, the grammatical balancing of opposite ideas. (c) He believes that the system contains *antithetical* elements which must resolve themselves into a synthesis. (d) A student must complete a hundred-page *antithesis* in order to win a degree.

EXERCISE 6C

Rewrite each of the sentences below, replacing the italicized word or phrase with a word from Word List 6 and writing the word in the form that fits the rest of the sentence. Use each word only once. Write your answers in the spaces provided.

1. The millionaire was a *person with peculiar ideas* and preferred to live in *dirty and disreputable* hotels.

   . . . .

   . . . .

2. "As happy as a couple just *engaged to be married*" is an example of a *literary comparison introduced by "as" or "like."*

   . . . .

   . . . .

3. The poor woman became *mentally ill* when she saw her husband's body placed in the *burial vault*.

   . . . .

   . . . .

4. He is *extremely clever* at making jokes, although his humor is somewhat *coarse and lacking in refinement*.

   . . . .

   . . . .

5. Here is a *short summary* of the article on the new *artificial fiber* fabrics.

   . . . .

   . . . .

6. The fast *rate of speed* of modern life does not suit everyone.

7. Are you so *willing to believe whatever you hear* that you accepted her promise to *send* the documents?

   . . . .

   . . . .

8. "Love, not hate" is an example of *the grammatical balancing of opposite ideas*.

   . . . .

   . . . .

9. A snake *moved with a rhythmical wavelike motion* across the clearing and ate and drank *in large quantities* at a small pond.

   . . . .

   . . . .

EXERCISE 6D

The word SYNTHETIC means "man-made; artificial" and is derived from a Greek prefix *syn-* (together) and a Greek root *thesis*, from the verb *tithenai* (to place; to put). Note that *syn-* becomes *syl* before *l* and *sym* before *b*, *m*, and *p*.

Complete the following words by adding the appropriate form of the Greek prefix that means "together." Give a brief definition of each word.

1. ___ PHONY . . . .

   . . . .

   . . . .

2. ___ AGOGUE . . . .

   . . . .

   . . . .

3. ____LABLE . . . .

. . . .

. . . .

4. ____CHRONIZE . . . .

. . . .

. . . .

5. ____METRY . . . .

. . . .

. . . .

6. ____DICATE . . . .

. . . .

. . . .

7. ____ONYM . . . .

. . . .

. . . .

8. ____PTOM . . . .

. . . .

. . . .

9. ____OPSIS . . . .

. . . .

. . . .

10. ____PATHY . . . .

. . . .

. . . .

EXERCISE 6E

Write out, in the spaces provided, the words from Word List 6 for which a definition, synonym, or antonym is given on the next page. When you are asked to give a root or a prefix, you should refer back to the preceding exercise; the information you require will be found there. Make sure that each of your answers has the same number of letters as there are spaces. A definition followed by a number is a review word; the number gives the Word List from which it is taken.

If all the words are filled in correctly, the boxes running down the answer spaces will continue the quotation begun earlier.

1. to arrange in order or degree (2)

2. behaving oddly; peculiar

3. a synonym for *abundant*

4. to produce young in large numbers (5)

5. an antonym for *sane*

6. coarse; lacking refinement

7. an antonym for *concrete*

8. a synonym for *opposite*

9. to punish, especially by beating (2)

10. an antonym for *clumsy*

11. a synonym for *artificial*

12. a pointed hand tool used for making holes (4)

13. a comparison introduced by *as* or *like*

14. made cheaply and insubstantially

15. to figure out the meaning of (1)

16. rate of speed, as in music

17. to move with a wavelike motion

18. a vault for burial; a tomb

19. an antonym for *suspicious*

20. a Greek prefix meaning "together"

21. engaged to be married

22. a synonym for *send*

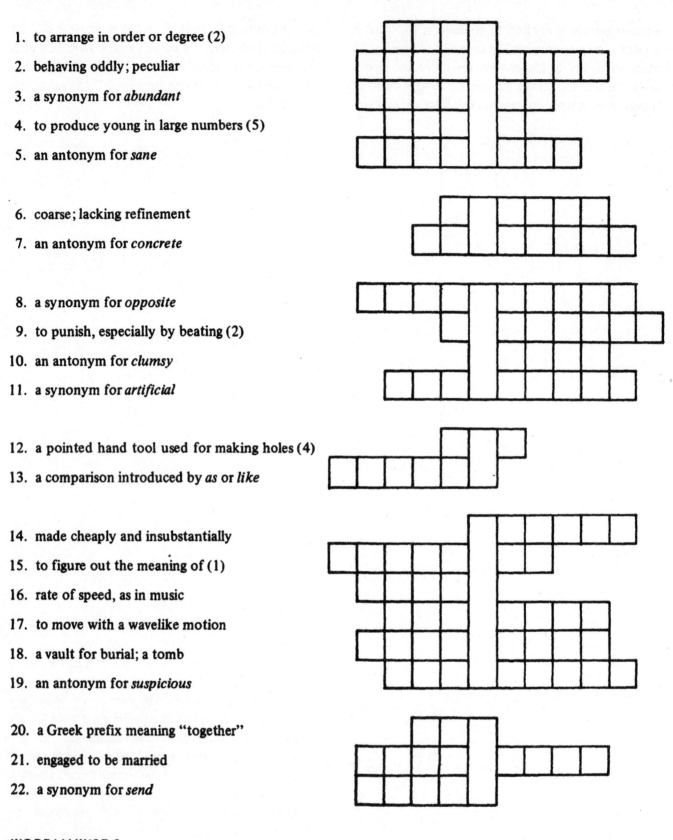

WORDLY WISE 6

CREDULOUS means "willing to believe without proof; easily deceived." Do not confuse this term with *credible*, which means "capable of being believed; reliable." Both words are derived from the Latin *credere* (to believe).

A *metaphor* is a figure of speech in which a

term or phrase is applied to something to which it is not literally applicable ("a tower of strength," "a heart of stone"). *Metaphors* are common in our daily speech and often get closer to the truth of things than literal statements do. The comparison in a *metaphor* is implied rather than stated. The SIMILE, however, is a more specific term in which the comparison is pointed out by the introduction of *as* or *like* ("as strong as a bull," "a voice like thunder").

ACROSS

1. one of a group taking the law into its own hands
6. willing to believe without proof
9. great mental and creative ability (2)
10. an official count of the population
12. a flexible, heelless leather shoe
14. incapable of being corrected
15. to specify as a necessary condition
18. a loose outer garment, especially as worn in ancient Rome
19. coarse food for animals
21. an intended partner in marriage
26. unwilling; opposed
27. protection or sponsorship (3)
28. to destroy completely
30. a comparison introduced by *as* or *like*
31. artificial; man-made
34. behaving oddly; peculiar
39. heavy bleeding
40. a feeling of being offended
42. an object prized for its scarceness (3)
44. a disease that rages unchecked
45. to compel by making threats
47. of good reputation; respectable
48. an understanding of the nature of something
49. to refuse to accept or acknowledge
50. an exact opposite

DOWN

1. bitterly spiteful and revengeful
2. that cannot be stopped or turned aside
3. to make a summary of
4. to move in a wavelike manner
5. to throw out; to expel
7. to send or pay (money)
8. to figure out the meaning of (1)
11. showing wisdom or shrewdness
13. a sharp pointed tool used for making holes
16. a woven fabric or cloth
17. the consequence (often unpleasant) of something (1)
20. to deny
22. coarse; lacking refinement
23. one who celebrates noisily
24. a sleeplike state
25. rate of speed, as in music
29. that can be touched; solid; real
30. shoddy; disreputable
31. a vault or tomb for burial
32. a quantity over what is needed
33. to produce young in large numbers
35. abundant; plentiful
36. feeling or showing love, respect, or awe
37. feeling or showing guilt or remorse
38. of unsound mind; mentally ill
41. agreement
43. highly skilled; expert
46. to help or encourage in wrongdoing

Chapter Three

Word List 7

ABRIDGED	DATA	GROTTO
ACRID	DISTEND	OVERSEER
ANNEX	EPISTLE	SQUEAMISH
BINOCULAR	FACTOTUM	SYMBOL
CARNAGE	FLAY	TRANSCRIBE

Look up the words above in your dictionary. Note that some of the words have more than one meaning. When you feel that you know *all* the meanings of *all* the words, go on to the exercise below.

EXERCISE 7A

From the four choices under each phrase or sentence, you are to mark the one that is closest in meaning to the word appearing in italics. When the same word appears more than once, you should note that it is being used in a different sense.

1. to enter the *grotto*
   (a) stream (b) cave (c) pool (d) wood

2. an *abridged* version
   (a) corrected (b) shortened (c) lengthened (d) banned

3. to deplore the *carnage*
   (a) suffering caused by famine (b) wholesale bribery of officials (c) deliberate burning of property (d) bloody killing of many people

4. Don't be so *squeamish*!
   (a) willing to tell tales (b) quick to judge people (c) easily upset (d) lacking in willpower

5. a general *factotum*
   (a) alarm (b) store (c) principle (d) handyman

6. to obtain the *data*
   (a) facts from which conclusions may be drawn (b) assurance of one's personal safety (c) sweet, fleshy fruit of the palm tree (d) key to a message written in code

7. to *annex* a territory
   (a) elevate to statehood (b) attach or join to a larger area (c) give independence to (d) break off relations with

8. a small *annex*
   (a) item for sale by auction (b) addition to something larger (c) advance patrol of an army (d) tax on imported goods

9. to replace the *overseer*
   (a) supervisor (b) main support (c) overhead structure (d) person who does odd jobs

10. to be *distended*
    (a) shriveled (b) lightened (c) swollen (d) looked after

11. *acrid* fumes
    (a) poisonous (b) sharp-smelling (c) intoxicating (d) invisible

12. *acrid* words
    (a) polite (b) many-syllabled (c) one-syllable (d) bitter

13. to *transcribe* the notes
    (a) make necessary corrections in (b) question the accuracy of (c) destroy (d) make a written copy of

14. a *symbol* of peace
    (a) brief period (b) object that is representative (c) act that marks the end (d) offer

15. to *flay* the deer
(a) remove the entrails from (b) remove the skin from (c) remove the antlers from (d) remove the head from

16. to *flay* someone
(a) willfully deceive (b) harshly criticize (c) inspire with courage (d) ally oneself with

17. *binocular* vision
(a) extremely good (b) of one eye (c) of two eyes (d) extremely poor

18. to read the *epistle*
(a) letter (b) warning (c) sign (d) heavy book

Check your answers against the correct ones below. The answers are not in order; this is to prevent your eye from catching sight of the correct ones before you have had a chance to do the exercise on your own.

6a. 11b. 16b. 4c. 1b. 12d. 17c. 3d. 15b. 18a. 13d. 9a. 8b. 10c. 2b. 7b. 5d. 14b.

Go back to your dictionary and look up again those words for which you gave incorrect answers. Only after doing this should you go on to the next exercise.

EXERCISE 7B
Each word in Word List 7 is used four times in the following sentences; one of the sentences in each group uses the word incorrectly. You are to circle the letter that precedes that sentence. Do not circle more than one letter in any one group.

1. (a) He was afraid his mother would *flay* him for losing the money. (b) She *flayed* the animal and stretched out the skin to dry. (c) The sailors leaped joyfully into the *flay* with fists flying. (d) The critics *flayed* my new book of essays.

2. (a) The *acrid* smell of gunpowder filled the air. (b) The liquid had an *acrid* taste like strong brine. (c) The *acrid* tone of her voice indicated that she was a very bitter woman. (d) The burned building presented a most *acrid* sight.

3. (a) We *annexed* a path through the snow with a pair of shovels. (b) Hitler's *annexation* of Sudetenland was one of the causes of World War II. (c) The guests were housed in the *annex* to the main building. (d) Texas was *annexed* to the Union in 1845.

4. (a) The pictures of the smokers' diseased lungs are not for the *squeamish*. (b) Persons attending the wounded at a military hospital soon learn not to be *squeamish* (c) She was not *squeamish* about accepting bribes. (d) This film is so *squeamish* that it is recommended for adults only.

5. (a) The club had roughly plastered walls and was lit to resemble a *grotto*. (b) Her voice sounded *grotto*, as though she had a bad cold. (c) The blue *grotto* at Capri can be visited only by boat at low tide. (d) A cave can be bare and simple, but a *grotto* is usually rocky and picturesque inside.

6. (a) The two lines appear to be equal in length, but this is a *binocular* illusion. (b) *Binocular* vision gives us much better depth perception. (c) A *binocular* microscope enables the observer to examine the specimen with both eyes. (d) *Binoculars* are more effective than a telescope because both eyes are used.

7. (a) You can take the letter down in shorthand now and *transcribe* it later. (b) If there is any dispute as to what was said, the court stenographer's *transcript* is accepted as final. (c) The alchemists of the Middle Ages tried to *transcribe* lead into gold. (d) Speech is *transcribed* accurately with phonetic symbols.

8. (a) The *overseer* had a hundred people working in the field. (b) The house is pleasantly situated

and *overseers* a large park. (c) One employee was chosen as *overseer* to supervise the work of the others. (d) Her job was to *oversee* the people placed in her charge.

9. (a) The *abridged* version of the novel runs to fewer than 200 pages. (b) Because of the decreased demand, library services are *abridged* considerably in the summer. (c) The sleeves are too long and will have to be *abridged*. (d) This 100-page *abridgement* preserves very little of the flavor of the original novel.

10. (a) Paul's *epistle* to the Corinthians is one of many letters he wrote to his followers. (b) Judas was one of the twelve *epistles* of Jesus. (c) Every week the mother penned a lengthy *epistle* to her daughter. (d) An *epistolary* novel is one written in the form of a series of letters.

11 (a) The lion is the *symbol* of courage. (b) A small cross is the *symbol* used on the map to show the location of my house. (c) She loved the rolling drums and clashing *symbols* of the band. (d) The wedding ring is intended to *symbolize* unending love.

12. (a) He was employed as a *factotum* around the ranch. (b) He was the general *factotum* for the village and was always being called on to do odd jobs. (c) Her job was that of a reporter, but she was employed as a kind of *factotum* around the office. (d) A small *factotum* was built to manufacture auto parts.

13. (a) The time by which you must return has been *distended* by an hour. (b) The *distended* beak of the pelican is used for storing food. (c) The profits of the industry are so *distended* that the government may soon step in. (d) Her stomach was *distended* from all the food she had eaten.

14. (a) We lack sufficient *data* to enable us to form any conclusion. (b) The *data* you require can be found in these tables. (c) The information provided by the computer is only as accurate as the *data* fed into it. (d) *Data* the facts so that you know they are accurate.

15. (a) The president appealed for an end to the *carnage* of war. (b) Doctors removed the *carnage* from his wound and put on fresh dressing. (c) The painting depicts the *carnage* of the battlefield at Gettysburg. (d) Peace came after four years of terrible bloodshed and *carnage*.

EXERCISE 7C

Rewrite each of the sentences below, replacing the italicized word or phrase with a word from Word List 7 and writing the word in the form that fits the rest of the sentence. Use each word only once. Write your answers in the spaces provided.

1. If you are *easily shocked or upset*, you should not look at the scenes showing the *bloody killings* of the battlefield.

   . . . .

   . . . .

2. After you *remove the skin from* the animal, stretch the skin out to dry.

   . . . .

   . . . .

3. He's merely the general *odd job person* at the ranch, but he acts as though he were the *person in charge of the hands*.

   . . . .

   . . . .

4. The *sharply bitter* smell of sulphur caused his nostrils to *stretch and swell out*.

   . . . .

   . . . .

41

5. The microscope is *designed for use by both eyes* so that specimens can be seen as solid objects.

   . . . .

   . . . .

6. The *smaller addition* to the club had been decorated to resemble a *rocky, picturesque cave*.

   . . . .

   . . . .

7. The *letter* which runs to over twenty pages has been *reduced in length* for publication.

   . . . .

   . . . .

8. A lion is an *object that stands as the representation* of courage.

   . . . .

   . . . .

9. I have assembled the *facts from which certain conclusions may be drawn*, and would like you now to *make a written copy of* my notes.

   . . . .

   . . . .

EXERCISE 7D

From the Latin *facere* (to do; to make) we derive the root *fac(t)*, also written *fic(t)* or *fec(t)*. This root forms the basis of many English words. FACTOTUM, for example, is formed from *fac* (do) and the Latin word *totum* (all) and means "a man who *does all* kinds of work."

Complete the following words, for which prefixes and suffixes have been supplied, by filling in the appropriate form of the Latin root that means

"do" or "make." Write out a brief definition of each word.

1. _____OR . . . .

   . . . .

   . . . .

2. EF_____IENT . . . .

   . . . .

   . . . .

3. _____ILE . . . .

   . . . .

   . . . .

4. _____ION . . . .

   . . . .

   . . . .

5. PRO_____IENT . . . .

   . . . .

   . . . .

6. PER_____ . . . .

   . . . .

   . . . .

7. EF_____IVE . . . .

   . . . .

   . . . .

8. _____SIMILE . . . .

   . . . .

9. DE___ . . . .

. . . .

. . . .

10. AF___ . . . .

. . . .

. . . .

EXERCISE 7E

Write out, in the spaces provided, the words from Word List 7 for which a definition, synonym, or antonym is given on the next page. When you are asked to give a root or a prefix, you should refer back to the preceding exercise; the information you require will be found there. Make sure that each of your answers has the same number of letters as there are spaces. A definition followed by a number is a review word; the number gives the Word List from which it is taken.

If all the words are filled in correctly, the boxes running down the answer spaces will continue the quotation begun earlier.

1. one who supervises the work of others

2. a smaller addition to a building

3. abundant; plentiful (6)

4. easily shocked or upset

5. of or involving both eyes

6. an antonym for *shrink*

7. considered apart from a concrete object (6)

8. a sign or object that stands for something else

9. of or relating to earliest times (2)

10. tooth or bone decay (3)

11. facts from which conclusions can be drawn

12. made of artificial materials (6)

13. sharp tasting or smelling; bitter

14. to move with a wavelike motion (6)

15. an antonym for *lengthened*

16. to remove the skin from

17. a person who does odd jobs

18. incapable of being corrected (4)

19. the bloody killing of many people

20. to compel by making threats (4)

21. a synonym for *letter*

22. engaged to be married (6)

23. a form of the Latin root meaning "make" or "do"

24. to make a written copy of

25. a rocky, picturesque cave

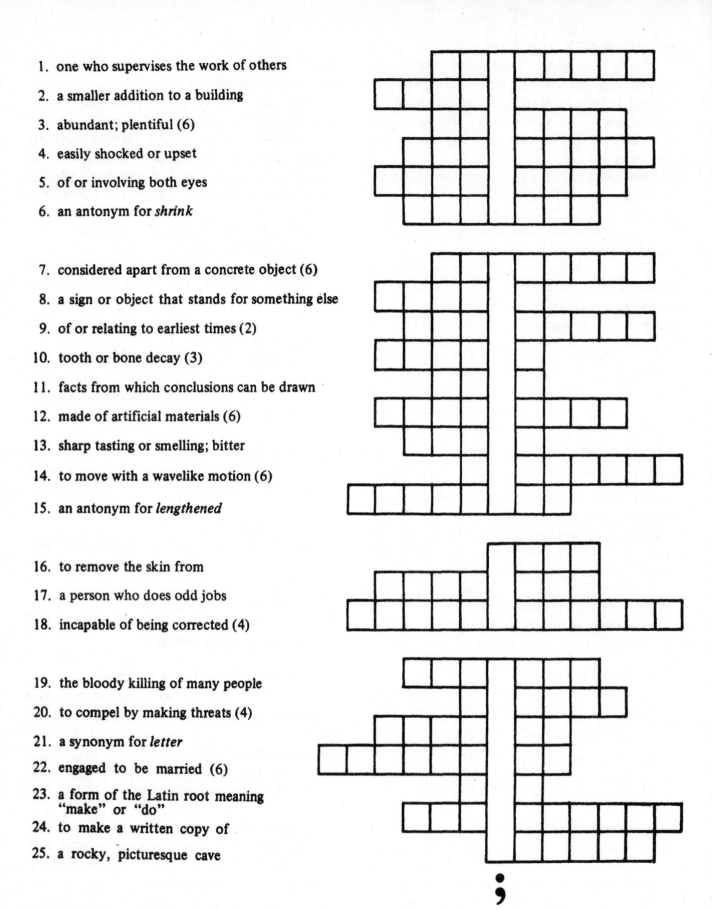

WORDLY WISE 7

DATA, meaning "facts from which conclusions can be drawn," is a plural term. Its singular form, which occurs less frequently, is *datum*. The plural and singular endings of this word indicate that it has been brought unchanged into English from Latin.

An EPISTLE is a letter; this term occurs frequently in the Bible (Paul's *epistle* to the Corinthians). A similar sounding term, also found in the Bible, is *apostle*, which means "a follower" (the twelve Apostles of Jesus).

The plural of GROTTO is usually written *grottoes*; however, *grottos* is also correct.

A SYMBOL is a sign or object that represents something else. (A white feather is the *symbol* of cowardice.) A homonym (see Introduction for an explanation of this term) of *symbol* is *cymbal*, a round brass plate used in orchestras and bands.

Word List 8

ALUMNI	CULL	REPREHENSIBLE
AMPHIBIAN	EXORBITANT	RESTITUTION
ARBITRARY	GULLIBLE	RESURGENT
BANDY	INTREPID	TITILLATE
CREDENCE	PANDER	TRANSPOSE

Look up the words above in your dictionary. Note that some of the words have more than one meaning. When you feel that you know *all* the meanings of *all* the words, go on to the exercise below.

EXERCISE 8A

From the four choices under each phrase or sentence, you are to mark the one that is closest in meaning to the word appearing in italics. When the same word appears more than once, you should note that it is being used in a different sense.

1. Volunteerism is *resurgent.*
   (a) rising again (b) likable (c) to be condemned (d) to be encouraged

2. an *amphibious* creature
   (a) that changes its form completely (b) that eats insects (c) that lays eggs (d) that lives in water and on land

3. an *intrepid* person
   (a) fearless (b) wise (c) ignorant (d) cowardly

4. an *arbitrary* decision
   (a) having the force of law (b) based on personal whim (c) arrived at after discussion (d) not binding on anyone

5. to *titillate* the masses
   (a) rouse to action (b) excite pleasurably (c) destroy the liberty of (d) raise the standards of

6. to lack *credence*
   (a) proper authority for something (b) belief in what another says (c) confidence in one's own ability (d) sufficient evidence to convict

7. the *alumni* of a university
   (a) graduates (b) teachers (c) undergraduates (d) traditions

8. to *bandy* gossip
   (a) forbid (b) exchange (c) love (d) overhear

9. somewhat *bandy*
   (a) overweight (b) round-shouldered (c) dishonest (d) bowlegged

10. *restitution* for what one has done
    (a) a full pardon (b) a making up (c) a deep regret (d) a lack of concern

11. to *transpose* the letters
    (a) reverse the order of (b) spell out (c) say out loud (d) write out

12. to *transpose* the music
    (a) make up as one goes along (b) steal and pass off as one's own (c) write in a different key (d) commit to memory

13. *reprehensible* conduct
(a) that cannot be explained (b) deserving of rebuke (c) worthy of praise (d) appropriate to the time and place

14. *exorbitant* prices
(a) reasonable (b) excessively high (c) falling (d) fixed

15. a *gullible* person
(a) much overweight (b) easily deceived (c) very small (d) untrustworthy

16. to *cull* the articles on a subject
(a) write (b) pick out (c) comment on (d) denounce

17. to *pander* to someone
(a) stand up bravely (b) offer cheap satisfaction (c) convey information (d) look up

Check your answers against the correct ones below. The answers are not in order; this is to prevent your eye from catching sight of the correct ones before you have had a chance to do the exercise on your own.

8b. 3a. 14b. 17b. 15b. 13b. 2d. 11a. 6b. 5b. 4b. 1a. 12c. 10b. 16b. 9d. 7a.

Go back to your dictionary and look up again those words for which you gave incorrect answers. Only after doing this should you go on to the next exercise.

EXERCISE 8B
Each word in Word List 8 is used four times in the following sentences; one of the sentences in each group uses the word incorrectly. You are to circle the letter that precedes that sentence. Do not circle more than one letter in any one group.

1. (a) She must have been very *gullible* to believe such a story. (b) She took advantage of their *gullibility* to sell the car for much more than it was worth. (c) He is *gullible* enough to buy the Brooklyn Bridge if someone offered it to him. (d) He is such a *gullible* that he believes everything he hears.

2. (a) She offered to help in any way she could as *restitution* for her past misdeeds. (b) She has a strong *restitution* and should recover quickly from the blow. (c) No amount of money can provide adequate *restitution* for the widow of the dead man. (d) He offered to make full *restitution* for the damage he had caused.

3. (a) She was merely the *titillate* ruler and had no real power. (b) The book is full of little incidents designed to *titillate* the reader. (c) Movies seem to have as their object the *titillation* rather than the instruction of the public. (d) The shoppers in the market exchanged *titillating* bits of gossip.

4. (a) We are at a loss to explain the *resurgence* of religious feeling in the country. (b) After decades of comparative peace, nationalism is *resurgent* in the country. (c) The patient's condition grew *resurgent* during the night. (d) In a sudden, *resurgent* burst of activity, the cats ran through the house.

5. (a) He is so simple that he allowed himself to be *culled* of all his money. (b) She has *culled* the best passages from her various books to make this interesting collection. (c) She *culled* the flock, separating the weak and sickly sheep from the rest. (d) I offered to go into the garden and *cull* some roses for her.

6. (a) He has been extremely *exorbitant* and has spent much more than he should have. (b) The new car models use *exorbitant* amounts of gas. (c) Because of the housing shortage, people have to pay *exorbitant* rents. (d) The more you give them, the more *exorbitant* become their demands.

7. (a) Don't *transpose* the "i" and the "e" in "weird." (b) The music should be *transposed* to a higher key to make it easier for them to sing. (c) She was not *transposed* to help us, so we did the job unaided. (d) Someone had *transposed* the names on the two adjoining doors.

8. (a) We loved to *bandy* gifts on her birthday. (b) The cowboy was quite *bandy* from curling his legs around his horse. (c) Whenever the two met, they would *bandy* compliments for the first few minutes. (d) She refused to *bandy* words with her accusers, preferring to maintain a dignified silence.

(a) Do not dignify gossip by giving it *credence*. (b) There is no *credence* whatsoever to support his story. (c) The fact that the letter is where she said it would be lends *credence* to her story. (d) I can place no *credence* in his story since I know him to be a liar.

10. (a) Who is the *arbitrary* chosen to settle the dispute between them? (b) The symbols employed are quite *arbitrary*, and others would do as well. (c) The decision was an *arbitrary* one that bore no relation to the facts that had been presented. (d) The divisions have been made quite *arbitrarily* and may need to be revised later.

11. (a) Frogs, toads, and salamanders are *amphibia*, intermediate in many respects between fish and reptiles. (b) The aircraft was an *amphibian*, able to land on the ground or on water. (c) Beavers are *amphibious* creatures, able to live on land or in water. (d) Her attitude was an *amphibious* one, neither for the proposal nor against it.

12. (a) The man *pandered* the rug severely to get the dust out of it. (b) She criticizes Hollywood producers who pander to the public by glorifying violence in their movies. (c) We must not *pander* to the shortcomings of students by lowering our standards. (d) These fan magazines that *pander* to the low tastes of the public are actually quite harmless.

13. (a) No voices were raised in protest against this *reprehensible* deed. (b) It was *reprehensible* of you to take advantage of him. (c) We were *reprehensible* of what might befall us in such a dangerous spot. (d) He was *reprehensibly* lenient in dealing with the culprits.

14. (a) An appeal for funds has gone out to the *alumni* of the college. (b) Of what university is he an *alumni*? (c) He is an alumnus of the college where his father and grandfather were *alumni*. (d) If she is an alumna of the university, she should join the other *alumni*.

15. (a) It required great courage to paddle the canoe through the *intrepid* waters of the rapids. (b) Amelia Earhart, lost in a flight across the Pacific in 1937, was an *intrepid* aviator. (c) In his younger days, he was an *intrepid* explorer of the South American jungle. (d) Only the most *intrepid* people would volunteer for such a dangerous mission.

EXERCISE 8C

Rewrite each of the following sentences, replacing the italicized word or phrase with a word from Word List 8 and writing the word in the form that fits the rest of the sentence. Use each word only once. Write your answers in the spaces provided.

1. I *picked out* about fifty names from the list of *graduates of the university*.

   . . . .

   . . . .

2. You must be very *easily deceived* to have paid such an *excessively high* price for that painting.

   . . . .

   . . . .

3. Your conduct was certainly *deserving of rebuke*, and you should do what you can to make *up for what you did wrong*.

. . . .

. . . .

4. They love to *exchange* gossip, but you should place no *belief* in what they tell you.

. . . .

. . . .

5. Hollywood should not *provide cheap satisfaction* to the public by offering movies designed solely to *excite pleasurably*.

. . . .

. . . .

6. Our choice of a leader should not be *based on personal whim*, because we need someone who is cautious yet *not afraid of physical danger*.

. . . .

. . . .

7. There is no doubt that an interest in gardening is *on the rise again* in this country.

. . . .

. . . .

8. Be careful not to *reverse the order of* the "i" and the "e" in "weird."

. . . .

. . . .

9. Frogs are *able to live on land or in water* and make their homes near ponds and marshes.

. . . .

. . . .

EXERCISE 8D

From the Latin *credere* (to believe), we derive the root *cred(o)* which is found in a number of words suggestive of belief or believing.

Complete the sentences below by filling in the missing word that has *cred(o)* as its root. Prefixes have been supplied where they will be needed. Use appropriate suffixes as needed.

1. Her . . . . was a simple one: to tell the truth at all times.

2. The new ambassador to the U.N. presented her . . . . to the president as soon as she arrived.

3. He does everything he can to dis . . . . me in the eyes of others.

4. He is able to perform in . . . . feats of strength.

5. She's such a . . . . person that she will believe almost anything.

6. I can place no . . . . in your story.

7. Although you didn't finish first, you put up a . . . . performance.

8. Her story lacks . . . . , and I cannot accept it.

9. His claim to have broken the record was received with in . . . .

10. She did not write the book, but she got . . . . for assisting with the research.

EXERCISE 8E

Write out, in the spaces provided, the words from Word List 8 for which a definition, synonym, or antonym is given on the next page. When you are asked to give a root or a prefix, you should refer back to the preceding exercise; the information you require will be found there. Make sure that each of your answers has the same number of letters as there are spaces. A definition followed by a number is a review word; the number gives the Word List from which it is taken.

If all the words are filled in correctly, the boxes running down the answer spaces will conclude the quotation begun in Exercise 5E.

1. unreasonable; excessive; too much

2. rising or tending to rise again

3. a making up for loss or wrongdoing

4. a large, wide-mouthed water jug (3)

5. an antonym for *commendable*

6. to offer cheap satisfaction

7. to pick out; to select and gather

8. to excite pleasurably

9. a Latin root meaning "believe"

10. to bleed heavily (5)

11. sharp tasting or smelling (7)

12. to exchange (words) lightheartedly

13. belief in what another says

14. the bloody killing of many people (7)

15. highly skilled; expert (6)

16. a burial vault or tomb (6)

17. easily deceived

18. graduates of a college or university

19. based on personal whim

20. living or functioning on land and in water

21. filled with sorrow or remorse (4)

22. to reverse the order of

23. a synonym for *bold*

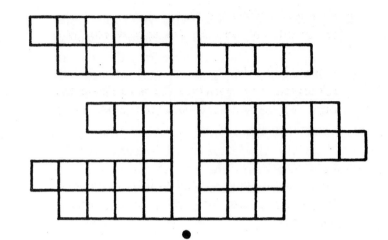

WORDLY WISE 8

ALUMNI is a Latin word which refers to the male or male and female graduates of a college or university. *Alumnae* refers to the graduates of a women's college and the female graduates of a coeducational college or university. Latin endings of gender are seen in the singular forms *alumna* (a female graduate) and *alumnus* (a male graduate).

AMPHIBIAN may be used as a noun or as an adjective, but it usually functions as a noun. *Amphibious* is the more common adjective form.

When BANDY refers to legs, it means that they "bend or crook outward." *Bandy-legged* or bowlegged mean the same thing.

Word List 9

ANNOTATED	CONSERVE	PERVADE
APPRAISE	EMBELLISH	SKIMP
BULWARK	HIDEBOUND	STALWART
CHASTEN	IMPASSIVE	STILTED
CONIFER	INAUGURATE	TREATISE

Look up the words above in your dictionary. Note that some of the words have more than one meaning. When you feel that you know *all* the meanings of *all* the words, go on to the next exercise.

EXERCISE 9A

From the four choices under each phrase or sentence, you are to mark the one that is closest in meaning to the word appearing in italics. When the same word appears more than once, you should note that it is being used in a different sense.

1. to *conserve* energy

(a) increase (b) save (c) lose (d) measure

2. apricot *conserves*
(a) pies (b) jams (c) puddings (d) drinks

3. to *embellish* something
(a) remove a part from (b) inquire into the nature of (c) add decorative details to (d) confirm the genuineness of

4. an *impassive* face
(a) flushed with anger (b) showing no feeling (c) dark and swarthy (d) covered with a veil

5. to *inaugurate* a service
(a) make improvements in (b) formally start (c) cut short (d) have need of

6. to *inaugurate* a president
(a) lay charges against (b) ceremoniously place in office (c) come immediately after (d) come immediately before

7. a *bulwark* against tyranny
(a) revolt (b) defense (c) speech (d) blow

8. a ship's *bulwarks*
(a) armed crew members (b) sides above the deck (c) sides below water (d) lower decks

9. to *skimp* on the job
(a) be in charge (b) spend as little as possible (c) take far too long (d) receive practical instruction

10. to *chasten* someone
(a) punish (b) reward (c) encourage (d) envy

11. *hidebound* ideas
(a) that are not properly thought out (b) narrow-minded and old-fashioned (c) universally accepted (d) dangerous and revolutionary

12. an *annotated* edition
(a) printed in limited numbers (b) signed by the author (c) cheaply printed (d) with explanatory notes

13. a large *conifer*
(a) cross section of a cone (b) cone-shaped mountain (c) evergreen, cone-bearing tree (d) cone-shaped, broadbrimmed hat

14. a *stalwart* person
(a) mean and underhanded (b) fearless and sturdy (c) extremely tall and thin (d) weak and undersized

15. a lengthy *treatise*
(a) agreement between nations (b) formal essay (c) scene in a play (d) episode in a story

16. *stilted* language
(a) deeply moving (b) forced and unnatural (c) spoken extremely fast (d) pleasing to the ear

17. to *appraise* a house

(a) make improvements in (b) belittle the worth of (c) demand a certain price for (d) estimate the worth of

18. to *appraise* a novel
(a) adapt for stage or screen (b) judge the quality of (c) sell to a publisher (d) circulate widely

19. to *pervade* the country
(a) win over (b) speak ill of (c) take by force (d) spread throughout

Check your answers against the correct ones below. The answers are not in order; this is to prevent your eye from catching sight of the correct ones before you have had a chance to do the exercise on your own.

3c. 13c. 19d. 1b. 16b. 18b. 4b. 6b. 15b. 8b. 14b. 17d. 2b. 11b. 5b. 12d. 10a. 9b. 7b.

Go back to your dictionary and look up again those words for which you gave incorrect answers. Only after doing this should you go on to the next exercise.

EXERCISE 9B
Each word in Word List 9 is used four times in the following sentences; one of the sentences in each group uses the word incorrectly. You are to circle the letter that precedes that sentence. Do not circle more than one letter in any one group.

1. (a) The ring was *appraised* by the jeweler at $450. (b) Why were we not *appraised* of your intentions? (c) Very few of the books *appraised* over the past year have been first class works. (d) The producer studied each of the dancers with an *appraising* eye.

2. (a) She has six *stalwart* children, each brave, reliable, and considerate. (b) The *stalwartness* of her supporters never wavered. (c) Both leaders are *stalwart* in their support of the proposed changes. (d) The *stalwarts* of the building were loose, and the roof was about to collapse.

3. (a) These animals are *hidebound* for the market. (b) Such a *hidebound* philosophy has no place in the modern world. (c) We should not allow ourselves to be *hidebound* by methods handed down from the past. (d) The senator's *hidebound* ideas of what is needed block all progress.

4. (a) The soldiers crouched behind the earth *bulwark* and awaited the attack. (b) A strong representative government is our best *bulwark* against tyranny. (c) As the ship rolled, the sailor staggered and fell against the *bulwarks*. (d) He was a *bulwark* young fellow, ready to give his life for his country.

5. (a) The title page of the book was *embellished* with an abstract design. (b) Tell the story as simply as you can and do not add any *embellishes* to it. (c) Her speech was *embellished* with an assortment of Latin phrases. (d) After being retold for the fifth time, the story had been considerably *embellished*.

6. (a) A judge who lacks fairness *pervades* the very idea of justice. (b) I hate the antiseptic smell that *pervades* hospitals. (c) A *pervasive* odor of decay clung to the old house. (d) An air of boredom *pervaded* the summer camp.

7. (a) She has completed her *treatise* on the rise of the nation-state. (b) A number of *treatises* on this subject have appeared in scholarly journals. (c) A peace *treatise* was signed by the warring nations. (d) The professor's *treatise* on the psychology of teenagers is a standard work on the subject.

8. (a) I received an *annotated* edition of Emily Dickinson's poems for my birthday. (b) He has agreed to *annotate* and write the introduction for this book. (c) The *annotations* to the text provide a wealth of useful information. (d) "I didn't care for the book at all," he *annotated* in reply to my question.

9. (a) Their training was *skimpy* and barely prepared them for their duties. (b) The builders managed to *skimp* nearly five thousand dollars off the cost of the new building. (c) They *skimped* on meals so that they would have enough money to buy tickets for the opera. (d) The *skimpiness* of the funds allotted to them made it impossible for them to do the job properly.

10. (a) His *impassive* features gave no indication of the pain he felt. (b) He stared *impassively* at us as we tried to explain why we were there. (c) It was impossible to tell from the *impassive* faces of the jurors what the verdict would be. (d) The heavy rains have made the road *impassive* to traffic.

11. (a) When people try to correct their speech, their pronunciation often becomes *stilted*. (b) After an hour's exercise my muscles are quite *stilted*. (c) "By word of mouth" is a *stilted* way of saying "verbally." (d) The figures in the painting appear *stilted* and unnatural.

12. (a) Maple trees begin to *conifer* in the fall. (b) Pine, spruce, and other *conifers* grew along the side of the hill. (c) *Coniferous* trees do not shed their leaves in the fall. (d) Fossilized pine cones indicate that *conifers* are a very ancient form of plant life.

13. (a) Many parents seem unwilling to *chasten* their children when they do wrong. (b) Imprisonment, not heavy fines, is the best way to *chasten* reckless drivers. (c) Being dropped from the team was a *chastening* experience for those who had missed practice. (d) The dish was of silver with a design *chastened* around its rim.

14. (a) The new ferry service was *inaugurated* yesterday with elaborate ceremonies. (b) The public's response *inaugurates* well for our proposal. (c) The *inauguration* of a new president takes place on January 20, following the November elections. (d) The president's *inaugural* ball is the social event of the season.

15. (a) We must *conserve* our strength for the battle that lies ahead. (b) She served a delicious *conserve* made of strawberries and rhubarb. (c) The *conservation* of our national forests is a matter of great importance. (d) Kruger National Park in South Africa is one of the largest game *conserves* in the world.

EXERCISE 9C

Rewrite each of the sentences below, replacing the italicized word or phrase with a word from Word List 9 and writing the word in the form that fits the rest of the sentence. Use each word only once. Write your answers in the spaces provided.

1. The *long formal essay* was written in very *stiff and artificial* English.

   . . . .

   . . . .

2. The soldiers crouched behind the *protective wall of earth and stones* and awaited the attack.

   . . . .

   . . . .

3. He was a *sturdy and resolute* fellow, and his face remained *without a trace of emotion* despite the strain he was under.

   . . . .

   . . . .

4. Our legal system is organized to *punish in order to correct* wrongdoers.

   . . . .

   . . . .

5. The book was *furnished with explanatory notes*, and the title page was *decorated* with the author's coat of arms.

. . . .

. . . .

6. The members are so *old-fashioned and narrow-minded* that they actually hate to see any changes.

   . . . .

   . . . .

7. We must *spend as little as possible* on repairs so that we may *save* what little money we have left.

   . . . .

   . . . .

8. An air of gaiety *was present throughout* the ceremonies that marked the *formal beginning* of the president's term of office.

   . . . .

   . . . .

9. He *estimated the value of* the stand of *evergreen cone-bearing trees* at about two thousand dollars.

   . . . .

   . . . .

EXERCISE 9D

Suffixes are commonly used to change the form of a word; they turn nouns into adjectives, verbs into nouns, and so on. They are used to form abstract nouns, to show whether a noun is masculine or feminine, to indicate size or degree, and to denote a quality or condition.

By supplying the missing suffix, complete the words in the following sentences. The roots have been supplied. Choose the suffixes from the following list and use each suffix only once.

-y	-or	-ly	-ose	-ion
-al	-ful	-tress	-ship	-ive

1. She used to be an act . . . . . but is no longer act . . . . . in the theater.

2. Carrot juice is an extremely health . . . . . drink, and a glass a day will keep you health . . . . .

3. She is an extremely verb . . . . . speaker, so I declined her verb . . . . . invitation to hear her give the talk.

4. He enjoys being an act . . . . . , especially if the play has lots of act . . . . .

5. She is a very friend . . . . . person and extends the hand of friend . . . . . to all she meets.

EXERCISE 9E

Write out, in the spaces provided, the words from Word List 9 for which a definition, synonym, or antonym is given below. When you are asked to give a root or a prefix, you should refer back to the preceding exercise; the information you require will be found there. Make sure that each of your answers has the same number of letters as there are spaces. A definition followed by a number is a review word; the number gives the Word List from which it is taken.

If all the words are filled in correctly, the boxes running down the answer spaces will give the first five words of a poem by Thomas Moore (1779-1852), the Irish national poet and scholar of Greek literature.

The poem will be continued in Exercise 10E.

1. sturdy and resolute

2. a creature able to live on land or in water (8)

3. to spread throughout

4. mentally unbalanced; insane (6)

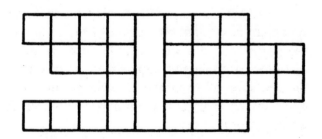

5. provided with explanatory notes

6. to send (6)

7. to spend as little as possible

8. a synonym for *save*

9. something that strengthens and protects

10. made of artificial substances (6)

11. one who does all kinds of work (7)

12. a synonym for *undemonstrative*

13. an antonym for *fluent*

14. old-fashioned and narrow-minded

15. a formal essay or prose work

16. to add decorative details to

17. to punish in order to correct

18. an evergreen, cone-bearing tree

19. to begin formally

20. to estimate the value or worth of

WORDLY WISE 9

APPRAISE means "to set a value on." Don't confuse this term with *apprise*, which means "to inform; to notify." (I *appraised* the house and its contents and *apprised* the owner of their worth.)

IMPASSIVE means "betraying no emotion." Its antonym is *animated*. Although the addition of the prefix *im-* to a word usually turns it into its opposite (possible and impossible), *passive* is not the opposite of *impassive*. *Passive* means "acted upon rather than acting; submissive" (a passive surrender, passive support).

Across

1. a making up for loss or wrongdoing
4. the bloody killing of many people
7. forced and unnatural
9. to offer gratification
10. an evergreen, cone-bearing tree
12. facts from which conclusions may be drawn
14. deserving of rebuke
17. provided with explanatory notes
18. a letter
21. one who supervises the work of others
22. to reverse the order of
25. something that strengthens or protects
27. the graduates of a college
29. easily shocked or upset
31. to exchange (words) lightheartedly
34. shortened; reduced in extent
36. to estimate the value or worth of
37. an object or sign that represents something
38. sturdy and resolute
39. fearless; bold
40. to keep from being used up
41. that can be touched or felt (5)
42. old-fashioned and narrow-minded
43. sharp tasting or smelling
44. a record of historical events (3)
45. to add decorative details to

Down

1. rising or tending to rise again
2. to spend or use as little as possible
3. showing no emotion
4. belief in what another says
5. a rocky, picturesque cave
6. to spread throughout
8. a formal essay or prose work
11. one who does odd jobs
13. to make a written copy of
15. of or involving both eyes
16. to attach or join to a larger area
19. to begin in a formal manner
20. too much or too great; excessive
23. to strip off the skin
24. to excite pleasurably
26. to make one's way; to travel slowly (2)
28. to punish in order to correct
29. made of artificial materials; man-made (6)
30. anything living or functioning on land and in water
32. to stretch and swell out
33. based on personal preference or whim
35. easily deceived
38. a comparison introduced by as or like (6)
40. to pick out; to select

Chapter Four

Word List 10

ABBREVIATED	ESCHEW	REMUNERATION
ACQUIESCE	IMPART	RIME
ASSIDUOUS	MANNERISM	SUAVE
DETRACT	NEBULOUS	VIRULENT
ENCLOSURE	RECOIL	WRIT

Look up the words above in your dictionary. Note that some of the words have more than one meaning. When you feel that you know *all* the meanings of *all* the words, go on to the exercise below.

EXERCISE 10A

From the four choices under each phrase or sentence, you are to mark the one that is closest in meaning to the word appearing in italics. When the same word appears more than once, you should note that it is being used in a different sense.

1. an annoying *mannerism*
   (a) attitude toward something (b) peculiarity of speech or behavior (c) inability to perform some task (d) refusal to cooperate

2. to *impart* flavor
   (a) lack (b) give (c) appreciate (d) possess

3. something to *impart*
   (a) hide (b) tell (c) remember (d) think about

4. a *suave* person
   (a) nervous and easily upset (b) sneaky and underhanded (c) bold and strong (d) gracious and self-assured

5. to *detract* from its beauty
   (a) derive inspiration (b) learn something (c) take away something (d) turn away

6. a *virulent* disease
   (a) highly infectious (b) mild (c) long-lasting (d) affecting certain animals

7. a *virulent* attack
   (a) ineffectual (b) long-awaited (c) surprise (d) hateful

8. *assiduous* labor
   (a) that has been replaced by machines (b) that is available at certain times only (c) marked by hard, steady effort (d) that can be hired cheaply

9. little *remuneration*
   (a) effort in one's work (b) payment for work done (c) understanding of what is required (d) ability to work alone

10. to *acquiesce*
    (a) rise to a higher position (b) agree without protest (c) protest strongly (d) drop to a lower position

11. an *abbreviated* version
    (a) authentic (b) fake (c) shortened (d) lengthened

12. to *eschew* something
    (a) shun (b) break up (c) remove (d) understand

13. to *recoil*
    (a) fasten together (b) spring back (c) leap forward (d) fall apart

14. to issue a *writ*
   (a) formal challenge to combat (b) notice announcing one's aims (c) document ordering or forbidding some action (d) license to engage in a trade

15. holy *writ*
   (a) writings (b) days (c) water (d) places

16. a large *enclosure*
   (a) crater made by a bomb (b) space shut in on all sides (c) opening into a courtyard (d) open, jagged wound

17. to read the *enclosure*
   (a) notice posted in a public place (b) material accompanying a letter (c) introduction to a book (d) short essay dealing with a single subject

18. covered with *rime*
   (a) dried mud (b) frozen mist (c) dust (d) confusion

19. The *Rime* of the Ancient Mariner
   (a) poem (b) adventure (c) plea (d) death

20. *nebulous* ideas
   (a) exciting (b) fully-developed (c) vague (d) useful

21. a large *nebula*
   (a) whale hunted for its oil (b) cloudlike group of stars (c) whirlpool caused by meeting currents (d) group of fish swimming together

Check your answers against the correct ones below. The answers are not in order; this is to prevent your eye from catching sight of the correct ones before you have had a chance to do the exercise on your own.

6a. 9b. 4d. 10b. 16b. 13b. 19a. 11c. 8c. 15a. 1b. 18b. 12a. 2b. 20c. 17b. 3b. 21b. 5c. 14c. 7d.

Go back to your dictionary and look up again those words for which you gave incorrect answers.

Only after doing this should you go on to the next exercise.

EXERCISE 10B
Each word in Word List 10 is used four times in the sentences below; one of the sentences in each group uses the word incorrectly. You are to circle the letter that precedes that sentence. Do not circle more than one letter in any one group.

1. (a) The common land was broken up by *enclosures* for the rearing of sheep. (b) With the letter there was an *enclosure* which I decided to read later. (c) The chickens were herded into a wire *enclosure*. (d) A check for fifty dollars was *enclosured* with the letter.

2. (a) Although he was a millionaire, he *eschewed* most of the luxuries of the rich. (b) She was a vegetarian and *eschewed* fish, flesh, and fowl. (c) They *eschew* violence, no matter how much they are provoked. (d) By hiding behind a low wall, she was able to *eschew* her pursuers.

3. (a) Coniferous trees keep their leaves in winter, but *assiduous* trees lose theirs. (b) He labored *assiduously* to complete the work by the required date. (c) Her *assiduous* efforts to sell the house were finally successful. (d) Even the most *assiduous* reviewer cannot hope to read all the books now pouring off the presses.

4. (a) His *suave* manners and elegant style of dress charmed the guests. (b) He tried to *suave* his conscience by sending money to the man he had wronged. (c) "I'm delighted to see you," she said *suavely*. (d) She conducted herself throughout the ordeal with such *suavity* that we were greatly impressed.

5. (a) He spoke haltingly and with many annoying *mannerisms*. (b) Pulling on her earlobe was one of her *mannerisms* that I remember. (c) I object to the content of her speech and not to the *mannerism* of its delivery. (d) An actor should adopt unconsciously the *mannerisms* of the person he is playing.

6. (a) The branches of the birch trees were *rimed* with frost. (b) Karl Shapiro's "An Essay on *Rime*" deals with modern poetry. (c) Her red-*rimed* eyes showed that she had had little sleep. (d) Old age had *rimed* his beard and dimmed his eyes.

7. (a) The court issued a *writ* forbidding the sale of the house. (b) The letter was *writ* the day before yesterday and mailed immediately. (c) The old preacher loved to quote holy *writ*. (d) He governed the territory by virtue of a *writ* from the queen.

8. (a) By trickery and other underhanded means, he *acquiesced* vast sums of money. (b) The others *acquiesced* without a murmur when he suggested surrendering. (c) She was obliged to *acquiesce* in the matter despite her misgivings. (d) She condemned the *acquiescence* of Congress in matters of foreign policy.

9. (a) Some doctors object to the *abbreviation* of their title to Doc. (b) For being absent from his post, the sergeant was *abbreviated* to the rank of private. (c) Most of the members of the band wore *abbreviated* costumes. (d) The novel has been simplified and *abbreviated* for young readers.

10. (a) This vaccine increases a person's *virulence* to the disease. (b) Bubonic plague is one of the most *virulent* diseases known. (c) The *virulence* of the speech he gave shocked even his own supporters. (d) The mosquitoes in this region are a particularly *virulent* breed.

11. (a) The herbs *impart* their flavor to the stew. (b) The father had grave news to *impart* to his children. (c) *Imparted* wines generally cost more than the domestic varieties. (d) Her air of authority *imparted* a seriousness to the proceedings.

12. (a) The spiral *nebula* in Andromeda is one of the great sights in the heavens. (b) The line between smart business practices and breaking the law can sometimes be a *nebulous* one. (c)

Her poetry brings into sharp focus the *nebulous* hopes and fears of the people. (d) His hearing is somewhat *nebulous*, but he refuses to wear a hearing aid.

13. (a) He *recoiled* in disgust when he saw the slugs in his driveway. (b) The rope had been *recoiled* neatly and put back in the locker. (c) Their hatred will surely *recoil* on themselves. (d) A *recoilless* rifle is one that does not kick back when fired.

14. (a) "I'd rather not," she *remunerated* hastily. (b) You will be adequately *remunerated* for your services. (c) He had a *remunerative* sideline selling produce from his garden. (d) If the work is interesting, she may be willing to work for little or no *remuneration*.

15. (a) A lack of balance in the painting *detracts* from its overall effect. (b) His position on this issue *detracts* from his reputation as a conservative. (c) As she had no proof, she was forced to *detract* her statement that the mayor had accepted bribes. (d) This chatter is meant to *detract* attention from the real issue.

EXERCISE 10C

Rewrite each of the following sentences, replacing the italicized word or phrase with a word from Word List 10 and writing the word in the form that fits the rest of the sentence. Use each word only once. Write your answers in the spaces provided.

1. A *legal order from the courts* was obtained by the author forbidding the publication of her book in *shortened* form.

. . . .

. . . .

2. The branches of the trees were covered with *white, frozen mist*.

. . . .

. . . .

3. She *agreed without protesting* when she was asked to work without *payment for the work done*.

. . . .

. . . .

4. A board fence had been erected to form a *space shut in on all sides*.

. . . .

. . . .

5. I do not wish to *say anything that would take away* from their efforts since they worked *long and hard* on the project.

. . . .

. . . .

6. He *carefully avoids* work in any form, and his plans for the future are extremely *vague and indefinite*.

. . . .

. . . .

7. Her manner is extremely *gracious and self-assured*, with no annoying *peculiarities of speech or behavior* to distract her listeners.

. . . .

. . . .

8. He *drew back* in horror at the *hostile and hateful* words of the speaker.

. . . .

. . . .

EXERCISE 10D

DETRACT, meaning "to take away from," is formed from the Latin prefix *de-* (from) and the root *tract*, derived from the Latin *trahere* (to pull; to draw).

To fill in the missing words in the sentences below, combine this root *tract* with an appropriate prefix or suffix from the following list:

Prefixes: *at-, dis-, ex-, pro-, re-, sub-, con-*
Suffixes: *-ion, -able, -or*

1. We hope the window display will . . . . a lot of attention.

2. Don't let the noise . . . . you from your studies.

3. I was nervous about riding, so they gave me a very . . . . horse.

4. The dentist will have to . . . . this abscessed tooth.

5. If you . . . . three from five, how many are left?

6. The wagon was hitched to the back of the . . . .

7. A . . . . is an instrument for drawing and measuring angles.

8. Did you . . . . to finish the job by the end of the month?

9. He was forced to . . . . his slanderous remarks.

10. Snow tires provide better . . . . than regular tires.

EXERCISE 10E

Write out, in the spaces provided, the words from Word List 10 for which a definition, synonym, or antonym is given below. When you are asked to give a root or a prefix, you should refer back to the preceding exercise; the information you require will be found there. Make sure that each of your answers has the same number of letters as there are spaces. A definition followed by a number is a review word; the number gives the Word List from which it is taken.

If all the words are filled in correctly, the boxes running down the answer spaces will continue the poem begun earlier.

1. a large system of stars taken as a group (1)

2. a synonym for *shortened*

3. a Latin root meaning "draw" or "pull"

4. white, frozen mist

5. sponsorship; protection (3)

6. a group of three closely related persons, being, or things (3)

7. a legal document ordering or forbidding some action

8. showing wisdom or shrewdness (4)

9. shoddy and disreputable (6)

10. gracious and self-assured

11. a synonym for *avoid*

12. a person who behaves differently (6)

13. a space shut in on all sides

14. an antonym for *harmless*

15. a synonym for *diligent*

16. to take away from something

17. a synonym for *payment*

18. to reveal; to share

19. an antonym for *definite*

20. to spring back

21. to agree to without protest

22. a peculiarity of speech or behavior

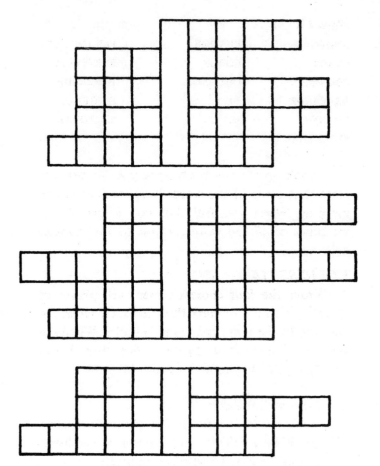

Word List 11

AMOROUS	EPITOME	PARAMOUNT
CHAOS	GORGE	PORTCULLIS
COMBINE	GUTTURAL	REPLENISH
DEMEANOR	HILT	RIGOROUS
DIVULGE	MIMIC	TEMPORAL
EPHEMERAL		

Look up the words above in your dictionary. Note that some of the words have more than one meaning. When you feel that you know *all* the meanings of *all* the words, go on to the exercise below.

EXERCISE 11A

From the four choices under each phrase or sentence, you are to mark the one that is closest in meaning to the word appearing in italics. When the same word appears more than once, you should note that it is being used in a different sense.

1. the *epitome* of grace
   (a) presence in all art (b) person or thing typifying a quality (c) person who shows a total lack (d) complete opposite

2. *ephemeral* pleasures
   (a) short-lived (b) forbidden (c) lifelong (d) social

3. the *paramount* issue
   (a) least important (b) most important (c) sadly neglected (d) much discussed

4. *temporal* affairs
   (a) unimportant (b) non-spiritual (c) not permanent (d) vitally important

5. a grave *demeanor*
   (a) crime (b) manner (c) error (d) decision

6. *amorous* words
   (a) soothing (b) hostile (c) loving (d) difficult

7. to *divulge* the facts
   (a) put together (b) discover (c) conceal (d) make known

8. the castle's *portcullis*
   (a) high tower that serves as a lookout (b) central courtyard (c) dungeon located far below ground (d) iron grating that closes off a gateway

9. to *gorge*
   (a) become angry (b) refuse firmly (c) become embarrassed (d) eat greedily

10. to approach the *gorge*
    (a) narrow, winding cave (b) deep, narrow pass (c) steep, flat-topped hill (d) wide, slow-flowing river

11. a jewelled *hilt*
    (a) headband (b) sword handle (c) ornamental cross (d) ceremonial belt

12. to *combine* them
    (a) force apart (b) make use of (c) bring together (d) put to work

13. an international *combine*
    (a) incident that causes war (b) group of business firms (c) agreement among states (d) code used by ships and planes

14. to operate a *combine*
    (a) crop dusting and spraying machine (b) spinning and weaving machine (c) ploughing and raking machine (d) harvesting and threshing machine

15. to *replenish* the stores
    (a) use up gradually (b) steal small amounts of (c) make a list of (d) provide fresh supplies of

16. a state of *chaos*
    (a) perfect peace (b) general uneasiness (c) utter confusion (d) sympathetic understanding

17. *rigorous* laws
    (a) unenforceable (b) outdated (c) fair (d) severe

18. *rigorous* study
    (a) strict (b) incomplete (c) preliminary
    (d) aimless

19. *guttural* sounds
    (a) high-pitched (b) foreign (c) familiar
    (d) deep-throated

20. to *mimic* someone's voice
    (a) record (b) imitate (c) listen for
    (d) recognize

Check your answers against the correct ones below. The answers are not in order; this is to prevent your eye from catching sight of the correct ones before you have had a chance to do the exercise on your own.

7d. 9d. 16c. 18a. 4b. 1b. 12c. 10b. 5b. 20b. 6c. 15d. 19d. 13b. 2a. 11b. 17d. 14d. 3b. 8d.

Go back to your dictionary and look up again those words for which you gave incorrect answers. Only after doing this should you go on to the next exercise.

EXERCISE 11B

Each word in Word List 11 is used four times in the following sentences; one of the sentences in each group uses the word incorrectly. You are to circle the letter that precedes that sentence. Do not circle more than one letter in any one group.

1. (a) Parrots are remarkably clever at *mimicking* human speech. (b) A small boy followed the soldier, *mimicking* his every movement. (c) She embezzled the money by *mimicking* the treasurer's signature on a check. (d) She was a clever *mimic* and would entertain us with imitations of famous people.

2. (a) The climate is so *rigorous* in winter that few venture out of doors. (b) She stared, *rigorous* with fear, at the horrible sight before her. (c) It takes years of *rigorous* study to become a doctor. (d) The judge applied the law so *rigorously* that she became known as "the hanging judge."

3. (a) The orange paint is a *combine* of red and yellow. (b) A dozen or so companies formed a *combine* to keep prices up. (c) A *combine* harvester cuts, threshes, and cleans grain while moving across the fields. (d) If we *combine* blue and yellow pigments, we get green.

4. (a) The castle's *portcullis* was lowered at nightfall to keep out enemies. (b) A *portcullis* was made of heavy iron grating suspended on chains. (c) The *portcullis* refused to open the gate for the strangers since he believed them to be robbers. (d) When the *portcullis* was dropped and the drawbridge raised, the castle was secure.

5. (a) The proud *demeanor* of the woman in the portrait suggests that she was a person of strong character. (b) Her sober *demeanor* contrasted with the gaiety of the other guests. (c) Do not *demeanor* yourself by associating with such disreputable characters. (d) His quiet, humble *demeanor* was in contrast to his fiery writings.

6. (a) The amount needed is so *ephemeral* that I am sure she will give it to us. (b) How *ephemeral* seem the pleasures of our youth when seen from the vantage point of old age. (c) Styles in popular music are *ephemeral* and quickly outdated. (d) The mayfly is an *ephemeral* creature, living for only a day.

7. (a) The room was in a state of complete *chaos*, with books and clothes strewn everywhere. (b) Traffic conditions in our cities grow more *chaotic* every year. (c) In the beginning was *chaos*, and out of this was created the ordered universe. (d) A *chaos*, fifty feet deep and a hundred feet wide, lay before them.

8. (a) The children *gorged* themselves on cakes and soda pop. (b) The bullfighter was badly *gorged* when he turned his back on the bull. (c) The *gorge* is very deep, and a small stream runs along the bottom of it. (d) The cruel way he treats his horses makes my *gorge* rise.

9. (a) The swans on the lake twine their necks in *amorous* play. (b) The soft lights and sweet music had put her in an *amorous* mood. (c) He *amoroused* the lady by proposing marriage on the day he met her. (d) The work is an *amorous* outpouring of the love of the poet for an unknown woman.

10. (a) The breakdown in service is *temporal* and will be resumed shortly. (b) He concerned himself with *temporal* matters, and left spiritual affairs to others. (c) The political rulers were quick to react whenever churchmen intruded in *temporal* affairs. (d) *Temporal* powers belonged to the king and the nobles, and spiritual power belonged to the bishops.

11. (a) Her final book was the *epitome* of a lifetime's thought and inquiry. (b) The British monarchy is the *epitome* of tradition. (c) The thoughtful leadership she offers *epitomizes* all that is best in her country. (d) The *epitome* on the tombstone was so old and weathered that I found it hard to read.

12. (a) Scottish people *guttural* the "ch" sound in words like "loch." (b) She spoke in a low, *guttural* voice. (c) The "g" in "go," and the "k" in "key" are *guttural* sounds. (d) He had difficulty mastering the *guttural* sounds in German.

13. (a) It was obvious that he had *replenished* a great deal of care on his car. (b) The innkeeper saw that the glasses of his guests were kept *replenished*. (c) Various fertilizers are used to *replenish* the soil. (d) The swimmers came to the surface to *replenish* their lungs with air, then dived to the bottom again.

14. (a) The property was mortgaged up to the *hilt*, and the bank refused to lend any more money on it. (b) She plunged the dagger into a large bundle and drove it in up to the *hilt*. (c) He gripped the *hilt* of his sword and drew it from its scabbard. (d) The two men *hilted* their swords as a gesture of friendliness.

15. (a) The reporter said she would go to jail rather than *divulge* the names of her informants. (b) She knew of the plot against the czar, but chose not to *divulge* it. (c) She read the statement carefully and did not *divulge* from it by a single word. (d) She did not *divulge* the contents of the letter to me.

16. (a) He was the *paramount* ruler of the tribes of the region. (b) She *paramounted* the throne at the age of seventeen and ruled for over fifty years. (c) The *paramount* problem of our time is the plight of our cities. (d) The need of the people to know the facts is *paramount* and overrides all other considerations.

EXERCISE 11C

Rewrite each of the sentences below, replacing the italicized word or phrase with a word from Word List 11 and writing the word in the form that fits the rest of the sentence. Use each word only once. Write your answers in the spaces provided.

1. His *manner of conducting himself* gave no hint that his feelings for her were *of a loving nature.*

. . . .

. . . .

2. Although the queen was the *supreme* ruler, her power was *concerned only with affairs of the world*, spiritual matters being left to the church.

. . . .

. . . .

3. He refused to *make known* the names of the companies that planned to *join together their operation.*

. . . .

. . . .

4. The young knight rapped the *handle* of his sword against the *iron grating that was lowered to close off the entrance* of the castle.

. . . .

. . . .

5. The two men *greedily stuffed* themselves with food and demanded that their glasses be *filled up again*.

. . . .

. . . .

6. Although its beauty is *of very brief duration*, the butterfly, while it lives, is the *creature that best typifies the qualities* of grace and lightness.

. . . .

. . . .

7. He tried to *imitate in a mocking way* the *deep-throated* voice of the guard.

. . . .

. . . .

8. The most *strict and severe* measures were adopted by the government to end the *state of complete confusion* that reigned in the country.

. . . .

. . . .

EXERCISE 11D

A number of English words are derived from the Latin *tempus*, meaning "time" and the Greek *chronos* meaning "time." TEMPORAL and *tempo* (Word List 6) are examples of words from the Latin.

Complete each of the following words with the appropriate Latin root *tempo* or the Greek root *chron(o)*. Prefixes and suffixes have been supplied. Then write a brief definition for each word. Check your dictionary for the correct spelling and the accuracy of your definition.

1. _____ LOGICAL

. . . .

. . . .

2. _____ RIZE

. . . .

. . . .

3. SYN_____ IZE

. . . .

. . . .

4. _____ RARY

. . . .

. . . .

5. _____ ICLE

. . . .

. . . .

6. ANA _____ ISM

. . . .

. . . .

7. _____ IC

. . . .

. . . .

8. EX _____ RANEOUS

. . . .

. . . .

9. CON _____ RARY

. . . .

. . . .

10. _____ METER

. . . .

. . . .

EXERCISE 11E

Write out, in the spaces provided, the words from Word List 11 for which a definition, synonym, or antonym is given below. When you are asked to give a root or a prefix, you should refer back to the preceding exercise; the information you require will be found there. Make sure that each of your answers has the same number of letters as there are spaces. A definition followed by a number is a review word; the number gives the Word List from which it is taken.

If all the words are filled in correctly, the boxes running down the answer spaces will continue the poem begun earlier.

1. relating to worldly or non-spiritual affairs

2. to make known

3. a Latin root meaning "time"

4. a synonym for *chief*

5. to spend as little as possible (9)

6. deep-throated; gruff

7. feeling or showing love

8. a person or thing typifying a quality

9. marked by hard, steady effort (10)

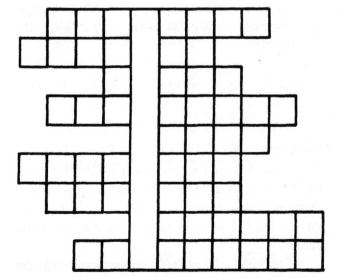

10. a sword or dagger handle

11. an antonym for *separate*

12. a Greek root meaning "time"

13. an iron grating lowered to close off an opening or gateway

14. total lack of order

15. to provide a fresh supply

16. to imitate, often in a mocking way

17. manner of conducting oneself

18. a synonym for *fleeting*

19. a deep, steep-sided, narrow pass

20. an antonym for *lax*

21. to exchange (words) lightheartedly (8)

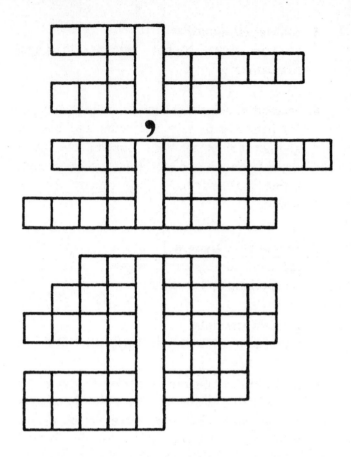

WORDLY WISE 11

AMOROUS and *loving* are synonyms, but note that *amorous* suggests romantic love (*amorous* glances exchanged by lovers) and is thus a more specific term than *loving*.

In addition to the meanings discussed in the exercises, GORGE can also mean "throat." In this sense it is used chiefly in the phrase "to make one's gorge rise," meaning to be filled with anger or disgust. (The way she treats those helpless animals makes my *gorge* rise.)

The word HILT is used metaphorically in the phrase *up to the hilt*, meaning "to the very limit, entirely, completely." (I can prove it up to the *hilt*.) This phrase is considered a cliché by some critics.

Word List 12

APPARITION	HERETIC	SENSUOUS
CLOISTER	LUCRATIVE	SNUB
COUNTERFEIT	MARTYR	TORPID
DELTA	PIOUS	UNDOING
FLUENT	PRUDENT	VOUCH
GINGERLY		

Look up the words above in your dictionary. Note that some of the words have more than one meaning. When you feel that you know *all* the meanings of *all* the words, go on to the exercise that follows.

EXERCISE 12A

From the four choices under each phrase or sentence, you are to mark the one that is closest in meaning to the word appearing in italics. When the same word appears more than once, you should note that it is being used in a different sense.

1. the *undoing* of someone
   (a) enforced departure (b) sudden death
   (c) bringing to ruin (d) sudden illness

2. the *undoing* of something
   (a) waste (b) end (c) cause (d) reversal

3. a *pious* person
   (a) very wealthy (b) very fat (c) extremely religious (d) extremely foolish

4. a *pious* rogue
   (a) hypocritical (b) malicious (c) wicked (d) likeable

5. *counterfeit* money
   (a) in coin (b) not genuine (c) paper (d) earned

6. accused of being a *heretic*
   (a) person who says one thing and believes another (b) person who opposes the teaching of his church (c) person who accepts bribes (d) criminal who cannot be reformed

7. to *vouch* for someone
   (a) stand in (b) accept payment (c) support by speaking up (d) search

8. *gingerly* attempts
   (a) hasty (b) timid (c) repeated (d) futile

9. *fluent* in the language
   (a) speaking with difficulty (b) expressing foreign words (c) able to speak easily (d) unable to speak

10. *fluent* verse
    (a) old-fashioned (b) smooth-flowing (c) difficult (d) unrhymed

11. to *snub* someone
    (a) rudely ignore (b) playfully hit (c) enlist the aid of (d) soundly defeat

12. a *snub* nose
    (a) pointed (b) flattened (c) short (d) large

13. to be a *martyr*
    (a) person who disagrees with the majority (b) person who dies for his beliefs (c) great religious or political leader (d) person who complains continually

14. to feel *torpid*
    (a) elated (b) sluggish (c) unwanted (d) hungry

15. a *lucrative* deal
    (a) profitable (b) illegal (c) private (d) fair

16. a *prudent* choice
    (a) final (b) wise (c) unwise (d) wide

17. *sensuous* music
    (a) that is repeated over and over (b) provided by a single instrument (c) that is made up as one goes along (d) that provides enjoyment to the senses

18. to see the *apparition*
    (a) real reason (b) ghostlike figure (c) true purpose (d) person standing guard

19. to enter the *cloister*
    (a) place of religious withdrawal (b) place of battle (c) tropical zone (d) brotherhood of monks

20. the columns of the *cloister*
    (a) invading army (b) front of a building (c) ruined building (d) covered walk

21. the *delta* of a river
    (a) total drainage area (b) total length from source to mouth (c) sand, mud, and other sediments (d) area of land at the mouth

Check your answers against the correct ones below. The answers are not in order; this is to prevent your eye from catching sight of the correct ones before you have had a chance to do the exercise on your own.

8b. 3c. 14b. 17d. 21d. 15a. 13b. 2d. 11a. 6b. 19a. 20d. 5b. 4a. 1c. 12c. 10b. 18b. 16b. 9c. 7c.

Go back to your dictionary and look up again those words for which you gave incorrect answers. Only after doing this should you go on to the next exercise.

EXERCISE 12B

Each word in Word List 12 is used four times in the following sentences; one of the sentences in each group uses the word incorrectly. You are to circle the letter that precedes that sentence. Do not circle more than one letter in any one group.

1. (a) The *cloistered* life of the scholar was not for him. (b) These nuns have chosen a life of worship and meditation within the *cloister*. (c) The people *cloistered* together in small groups. (d) The *cloister* ran around an open court and was walled on one side, with rows of stone columns on the other.

2. (a) The fish can survive the cold water but grow *torpid* as the temperature drops. (b) The enormous meal he had just consumed accounted for his *torpidness*. (c) The walls were painted a *torpid* grayish color. (d) It is impossible to reach the *torpid* minds of these students.

3. (a) The poor woman has been a *martyr* to rheumatism for thirty years. (b) A sheep was led to the altar and *martyred* by the high priest. (c) The early Christians suffered *martyrdom* in the Roman arena. (d) Sir Thomas More was *martyred* when he refused to bend to the wishes of Henry VIII.

4. (a) Hamlet is convinced that the *apparition* he sees is his father's ghost. (b) Promptly at midnight the *apparition* appeared on the castle battlements. (c) Was the figure an *apparition*, or does it have some natural explanation? (d) The ghost suddenly *apparitioned* out of the darkness.

5. (a) For supporting such advanced ideas, she was branded a *heretic*. (b) The animals saw that they were trapped and became extremely *heretical*. (c) Martin Luther openly defied the Catholic church and was tried for *heresy*. (d) She had better keep such *heretical* ideas to herself, or she will find herself in trouble.

6. (a) She is such a *snub* that she refuses to speak to those she considers inferior. (b) The little boy was *snub*-nosed with lots of freckles and red hair. (c) She ignored me when I greeted her, and I have no idea as to the cause of the *snub*. (d) I don't know why he *snubbed* you when you addressed him.

7. (a) The actress spoke her lines with great *fluency*. (b) She is *fluent* in German and French. (c) The smooth sides of the channel make for a more *fluent* movement of the liquid. (d) Alcohol is a *fluent* that freezes at a very low temperature.

8. (a) The two men were charged with passing *counterfeit* money. (b) I *counterfeited* her objection with good reasons for my plan. (c) The sorrow she expressed seemed *counterfeit*. (d) The gang had been *counterfeiting* $10 bills for some weeks before they were caught.

9. (a) The *delta* country of Mississippi is famous for its rich soil. (b) The rich soil of the Nile *delta* gave rise to one of the earliest civilizations on earth. (c) A *delta* is formed of sediment deposited at the mouth of a river. (d) The *delta* flows into the parent river about three miles upstream.

10. (a) She decided it would be *prudent* for her to keep the money in a safe. (b) She had not *prudence* enough to hold her tongue in front of the others. (c) The soil is extremely *prudent* in this region due to the heavy rainfall. (d) They *prudently* decided to drop the plan when they saw how strongly it was opposed.

11. (a) He is such a *lucrative* man, never happy unless he is making money. (b) She has a *lucrative* business selling computers. (c) The publishing of books of poetry is not a *lucrative* undertaking. (d) Perhaps the most *lucrative* deal in history was Queen Isabella's financing of Columbus' voyage.

12. (a) He was an extremely *pious* man and tried to live in accordance with the Koran. (b) They covered up their misdeeds with *pious* pronouncements about service to the community. (c) He was made a *pious* in the church at a very early age. (d) She was a woman of unquestioned *piety* and attended church regularly.

13. (a) The film used in today's cameras is extremely *sensuous* to light. (b) Mild, *sensuous* breezes, laden with the scent of pine, blew across the lake. (c) Her writing has a fine *sensuous* quality that lets you feel and see what she is describing. (d) She lowered herself into the warm, *sensuous* waters of the lagoon.

14. (a) He *gingerly* began to examine the bomb to determine whether or not it was live. (b) The drink had a sharp, *gingerly* taste that I liked. (c) She made her way *gingerly* over the ice, terrified that it would give way beneath her. (d) The issue was handled in *gingerly* fashion to avoid hurting anyone's feelings.

15. (a) Fill out a petty cash *vouch*, stating the amount of money needed. (b) The facts were assembled so quickly that I cannot *vouch* for their accuracy. (c) I can *vouch* for the truth of what she says. (d) Is there anyone here who can *vouch* for this man's honesty?

16. (a) He had been a promising lawyer, but he began ignoring his clients and that was his *undoing*. (b) The terrible ambition of Macbeth was his *undoing*. (c) Her *undoing* efforts have almost ruined the company. (d) She would settle for nothing less than the complete *undoing* of her team's defeat.

EXERCISE 12C

Rewrite each of the following sentences, replacing the italicized word or phrase with a word from Word List 12 and writing the word in the form that fits the rest of the sentence. Use each word only once. Write your answers in the spaces provided.

1. The *ghostlike figure* was seen at one end of the *covered walk that runs along the inside wall of the monastery*.

. . . .

. . . .

2. The *triangular area of land formed at the mouth* of the Mississippi River is noted for its rich soil.

. . . .

. . . .

3. By being *wisely cautious in what he did* with his money, he was soon able to build up a *profitable* business.

. . . .

. . . .

4. She is *able to converse easily* in French and German.

. . . .

. . . .

5. I am prepared to *speak up in support* for him, as I do not believe that he is a *person who opposes the views of his church*.

. . . .

. . . .

6. She greeted us *in a careful and timid manner*, afraid that we would *rudely ignore* her again.

. . . .

. . . .

7. Her attempt to pass money she knew was *not genuine* proved to be her *downfall*.

. . . .

. . . .

8. He was a *person who suffered death for his beliefs,* yet he remained *intensely devoted to his religion* to the very end.

. . . .

. . . .

9. The water is warm and *provides great pleasure to the senses,* but it leaves you feeling *sluggish and inactive.*

. . . .

. . . .

EXERCISE 12D

This exercise is a review of roots and prefixes covered so far. Underline the prefix in each of the words below. Give the meaning of each prefix and write two words having the same prefix.

1. expel . . . .

. . . .

. . . .

2. symphony . . . .

. . . .

. . . .

3. amorphous . . . .

. . . .

. . . .

4. abdicate . . . .

. . . .

. . . .

Underline the root in each of the following words.

Give the meaning of each root and write two words having the same root.

5. tractor . . . .

. . . .

. . . .

6. terminate . . . .

. . . .

. . . .

7. chronic . . . .

. . . .

. . . .

8. credible . . . .

. . . .

. . . .

9. factory . . . .

. . . .

. . . .

10. primitive . . . .

. . . .

. . . .

EXERCISE 12E

Write out, in the spaces provided, the words from Word List 12 for which a definition, synonym, or antonym is given on the next page. When you are asked to give a root or a prefix, you should refer back to the preceding exercise; the information you require will be found there. Make sure that each of your answers has the same number of letters as there are spaces. A definition followed by a number is a review word; the number gives the Word List from which it is taken.

If all the words are filled in correctly, the boxes running down the answer spaces will continue the poem begun earlier.

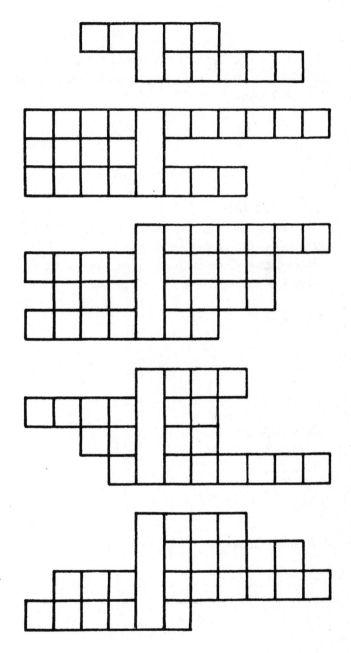

1. deeply religious

2. able to converse easily

3. an antonym for *genuine*

4. to give personal assurance

5. in a careful and timid manner

6. wisely cautious in what one does

7. a synonym for *profitable*

8. giving physical pleasure

9. one who opposes officially held beliefs

10. a legal document forbidding or ordering some action (10)
11. a bringing to ruin

12. a triangular area of land formed at a river mouth
13. a place of religious seclusion and withdrawal

14. to ignore rudely

15. a synonym for *sluggish*

16. a ghostlike figure

17. one who dies for his beliefs

WORDLY WISE 12

Note that GINGERLY is both an adjective (a *gingerly* attempt) and an adverb (to hold it *gingerly*).

The word MARTYR is used loosely to refer to one who sacrifices his life in a noble cause (the martyred president) or to one who suffers a great deal, as from disease (a martyr to rheumatism). Strictly speaking, it means "one who willingly accepted death for refusing to renounce his beliefs." (Stephen was the first Christian martyr.)

SENSUOUS and *sensual* both mean "appealing or gratifying to the senses rather than to the mind." However, *sensuous* suggests a more refined feeling of pleasure (*sensuous* music); *sensual* suggests a coarse feeling or overindulgence in base appetites (the *sensual* pleasures of the glutton). *Sensory* is a scientific term and means "of or relating to sensation or to the senses" (*sensory* nerve endings).

ACROSS

1. to provide a fresh supply of
5. short-lived; fleeting
10. white frozen mist
11. to eat greedily and to excess
12. an iron grating to close off a gateway
14. producing wealth or profit
15. payment for work done
18. to give assurances or support
19. to agree to without protest
21. providing pleasure to the senses
24. an area of uncultivated land, common in Scotland
26. having or pretending to have religious devotion
27. to come or bring together
30. total lack of order; utter confusion
31. a strong support or defense (9)
32. wisely cautious in what one does
37. to make known
38. to draw out; to bring forth (2)
39. a peculiarity of language or behavior
42. a ghostlike figure; a phantom
44. to draw or spring back
46. a person or thing typifying a quality
47. pertaining to worldly rather than spiritual matters
48. to believe; to consider (3)
49. deep-throated; gruff
50. to take away from

DOWN

1. strict; severe
2. first in importance; chief
3. to reveal or give
4. one opposing the beliefs of his church
5. material accompanying a letter
6. a sword or dagger handle
7. feeling or showing love
8. to imitate, often mockingly
9. manner of conduct
13. gracious and self-assured
16. vague; indefinite
17. to avoid; to shun
19. marked by hard, steady effort
20. able to converse easily
22. coarse; lacking refinement (6)
23. timidly careful
25. shortened
28. to ignore in a rude manner
29. not genuine; fake
33. highly infectious and deadly
34. a place of religious seclusion
35. a feeling of being offended (4)
36. a bringing to ruin
40. one who died for his beliefs
41. sluggish; inactive
43. a triangular area of land formed at the mouth of a river
45. a legal document ordering or forbidding some action

Chapter Five

Word List 13

ABNORMAL	FORETELL	ORGY
BLEAK	GAUNTLET	SOLAR
CONSECUTIVE	HETERODOX	THWART
DOUGHTY	INCONGRUOUS	TRANSIENT
EFFACE	MYRIAD	YOKEL
ENNUI		

Look up the words above in your dictionary. Note that some of the words have more than one meaning. When you feel you know *all* the meanings of *all* the words, go on to the exercise below.

EXERCISE 13A

From the four choices under each phrase or sentence, you are to mark the one that is closest in meaning to the word appearing in italics. When the same word appears more than once, you should note that it is being used in a different sense.

1. to *foretell* something
   (a) tell before it happens (b) tell from memory (c) try to hide (d) show by pointing at

2. *consecutive* days
   (a) chosen at random (b) following in regular order (c) set aside for a special purpose (d) odd-numbered

3. a *bleak* future
   (a) distant (b) exciting (c) unknown (d) gloomy

4. a *bleak* wind
   (a) gentle (b) harsh (c) warm (d) strong

5. a *bleak* place
   (a) attractive (b) desolate (c) faraway (d) small

6. *heterodox* views
   (a) outdated (b) religious (c) generally accepted (d) not generally accepted

7. to *efface* the letters
   (a) erase (b) underline (c) ink in (d) indicate

8. to *efface* oneself
   (a) talk at length about (b) hold a high opinion of (c) remove from notice (d) hold a low opinion

9. *abnormal* amounts
   (a) large (b) unusual (c) typical (d) small

10. He looks like a *yokel*.
    (a) reliable and hardworking person (b) private detective (c) gullible country fellow (d) spy

11. to *thwart* the attempt
    (a) make (b) block (c) encourage (d) pretend to make

12. to overcome his *ennui*
    (a) boredom (b) fault (c) handicap (d) unwillingness

13. *transient* pleasures
    (a) harmless (b) forbidden (c) short-lived (d) long-remembered

14. to be a *transient*
    (a) person with but a short time to live (b) person not legally an adult (c) person who travels to and from work (d) person who stays briefly and moves on

15. to seem *incongruous*
    (a) not noticeable (b) not important (c) not going well together (d) not leading to definite results

16. *solar* energy
    (a) potential (b) of the atom (c) of the sun (d) of motion

17. a Roman *orgy*
    (a) public holiday (b) large, public bath (c) official in charge of troops (d) wild, abandoned merrymaking

18. an *orgy* of eating
    (a) reasonable amount (b) complete avoidance (c) hearty dislike (d) excessive indulgence

19. *myriad* items
    (a) countless (b) urgent (c) unimportant (d) several

20. a *doughty* partner
    (a) weak and ineffectual (b) stupid (c) bold and strong (d) cunning

21. to wear *gauntlets*
    (a) long, protective gloves (b) shoulder armor (c) high boots (d) spurs

Check your answers against the correct ones below. The answers are not in order; this is to prevent your eye from catching sight of the correct ones before you have had a chance to do the exercise on your own.

15c. 4b. 8c. 7a. 17d. 12a. 18d. 6d. 1a. 10c. 21a. 11b. 2b. 5b. 20c. 13c. 14d. 16c. 19a. 3d. 9b.

Go back to your dictionary and look up again those words for which you gave incorrect answers. Only after doing this should you go on to the next exercise.

EXERCISE 13B

Each word in Word List 13 is used four times in the following sentences; one of the sentences in each group uses the word incorrectly. You are to circle the letter that precedes that sentence. Do not circle more than one letter in any one group.

1. (a) *Myriads* of insects, attracted by the light, swarmed about the porch. (b) A biographer cannot hope to recount all the *myriad* events of his subject's life. (c) The statue had been carved out of a solid piece of *myriad*. (d) She was beset with a *myriad* of problems, each demanding her immediate attention.

2. (a) Nothing could shake off the *ennui* that hung over them. (b) The more she tried to entertain the children, the more *ennui* they became. (c) The *ennui* she felt was mainly a result of her dull job. (d) The moment we become involved in the problems of others, all our cares and *ennuis* disappear.

3. (a) Time has *effaced* much of the detail of these famous cave paintings. (b) You must *efface* up to your responsibilities. (c) A year of rest had *effaced* the lines of worry from her face. (d) He is so modest that he *effaced* himself from the party in his honor.

4. (a) Everything happened exactly as the fortune teller had *foretold*. (b) She was able to *foretell* the weather with amazing accuracy. (c) Astronomers learned long ago to *foretell* the exact time of an eclipse. (d) With three players injured, our defeat in the game was a *foretold* conclusion.

5. (a) They *orgied* themselves with so much food that they became sick. (b) The Greeks worshiped Bacchus, the god of wine, by holding drunken *orgies* in his honor. (c) The senator engaged in a veritable *orgy* of speech-making before the election. (d) The *orgiastic* feasts of the Emperor Nero scandalized the respectable citizens of Rome.

6. (a) A television set in a play about Queen Victoria would be a noticeable *incongruity*. (b) She looked *incongruously* at me as though she didn't understand what I had said. (c) He was discharged from the army because his antiwar activity was *incongruous* with a career in the military. (d) He was an absurdly *incongruous* figure in his top hat and dungarees.

7. (a) She had spent her life in the country surrounded by *yokels* and was not used to city ways. (b) Many of the soldiers were *yokels* who had come straight from the plow. (c) The *yokel* who arrived in the city for the first time was naturally bewildered. (d) I'm learning how to *yokel*, but I can't change my voice quickly enough to get the sound right.

8. (a) The sheep gave a *bleaking* sound as it was led out of the pen. (b) The *bleak* wastes of the arctic are not habitable by humans without special protection. (c) A *bleak* wind rose, cutting into them and chilling them to the bone. (d) The future looks *bleak* for those who drop out of school without graduating.

9. (a) The men wore leather *gauntlets* to protect their hands and wrists. (b) The men formed two lines and, armed with heavy clubs, made their victim run the *gauntlet* between them. (c) He threw down the *gauntlet*, but none dared accept his challenge. (d) He threatened to *gauntlet* his opponent unless he surrendered.

10. (a) She made a model of the *solar* system showing the planets in relation to the sun. (b) A *solar* battery converts energy from the sun into electricity. (c) Amelia Earhart was the first woman to fly *solar* across the Atlantic. (d) A *solar* eclipse occurs when the moon passes directly in front of the sun.

11. (a) The Congress has enormous power to *thwart* the president. (b) They raised so many *thwarts* to my plan that I dropped the idea. (c) I did not wish to *thwart* him by raising too many objections. (d) Attempts to seize the royal palace were *thwarted* by the queen's guard.

12. (a) She *heterodoxed* those with whom she disagreed. (b) The rabbi's views are somewhat *heterodox* and are a source of concern to the congregation. (c) Anyone who has been taught in an orthodox manner would find the *heterodox* methods used here quite bewildering. (d) Medical societies do not encourage *heterodoxy* in the methods of their members.

13. (a) The bread seemed *doughty*, as though it had not been baked properly. (b) He was a *doughty* little fighter, not afraid to take on someone twice his size. (c) The soldiers fought *doughtily*, and by the day's end they had won the battle. (d) The young knight wished to prove himself as *doughty* a warrior as his father.

14. (a) She stayed at a cheap hotel which catered chiefly to *transients*. (b) The effects of the enemy occupation proved to be *transient* and quickly forgotten. (c) To change from a developing nation to a modern industrial state is a difficult *transient*. (d) *Transient* workers gradually move north as the various crops become ready for harvesting.

15. (a) It is certainly *abnormal* for an adult to require twelve hours of sleep a night. (b) Marked *abnormals* in behavior indicate that the services of a psychiatrist may be needed. (c) Temperatures have been *abnormally* low this past winter. (d) The doctor noted a number of *abnormalities* in the patient's behavior.

16. (a) For five *consecutive* days the storm raged. (b) President Roosevelt was elected to four *consecutive* terms of office. (c) We were asked to write down any three *consecutive* numbers, such as 3, 4, 5. (d) She was *consecutively* dressed in striped pants, jacket, and hat.

EXERCISE 13C

Rewrite each of the following sentences, replacing the italicized word or phrase with a word from Word List 13 and writing the word in the form that fits the rest of the sentence. Use each word only once. Write your answers in the spaces provided.

1. The *bold, strong* warrior removed his *heavy protective glove* and threw it to the ground.

   . . . .

   . . . .

2. This *sun-powered* battery has a *large number* of uses.

   . . . .

   . . . .

3. It seems *strangely out of place* that a *wild and uncontrolled merrymaking* was a part of the religious service of the ancient Greeks.

   . . . .

   . . . .

4. The *feeling of boredom and weariness* that hung over them proved to be *of very brief duration.*

   . . . .

   . . . .

5. Don't allow that *gullible fellow from the country* to *get in the way of* your plans.

   . . . .

   . . . .

6. A person whose opinions were in any way *different from the accepted view* was regarded as *being out of the ordinary.*

   . . . .

   . . . .

7. You must try to *wipe out* the memory of those *grim and cheerless* days you spent in the hospital.

. . . .

. . . .

8. How was she able to *tell ahead of time* that the five numbers would be *in unbroken numerical order?*

   . . . .

   . . . .

EXERCISE 13D

The word TRANSIENT is formed from the Latin prefix *trans-* (across) and a form of the Latin verb *ire* (to go). This prefix occurs in a number of English words.

Fill in the blanks in the sentences below with a word which begins with the prefix *trans-.*

1. The patient is hemorrhaging and needs a blood . . . .

2. . . . . flights between London and New York take about six hours.

3. We dug up the bushes and . . . . them to the front garden.

4. I was asked to . . . . the passage into French.

5. The banks do not . . . . business on Columbus Day.

6. The company has decided to . . . . him to the New York office.

7. This radio station . . . . on a frequency of 90.4 megacycles.

8. The alchemists of the Middle Ages tried to . . . . base metals into gold.

9. Supplies were . . . . to the site in five-ton trucks.

10. The limousine is fitted with a . . . .
. . . . top so that the crowds can see
the president.

EXERCISE 13E

Write out, in the spaces provided, the words
from Word List 13 for which a definition, synonym, or antonym is given below. When you are
asked to give a root or a prefix, you should refer
back to the preceding exercise; the information
you require will be found there. Make sure that
each of your answers has the same number of
letters as there are spaces. A definition followed by
a number is a review word; the number gives the
Word List from which it is taken.

If all the words are filled in correctly, the
boxes running down the answer spaces will conclude the poem begun in Exercise 9E.

1. a synonym for *cheerless*

2. departing from what is normal or usual

3. a large number

4. the handle of a dagger or sword (11)

5. a heavy, protective leather glove

6. of or relating to the sun

7. to remove; to wipe out

8. a wild, uncontrolled merrymaking

9. bold and strong

10. differing from the accepted view

11. a synonym for *predict*

12. a simple country fellow

13. an antonym for *permanent*

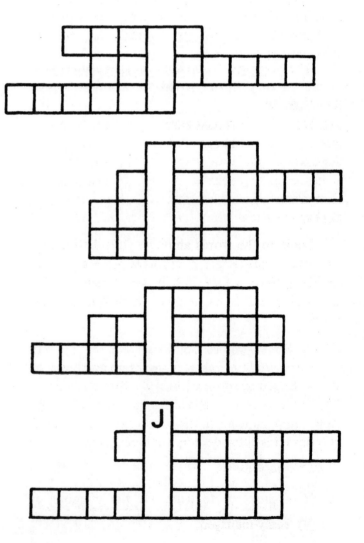

14. a Latin prefix meaning "across"

15. following in order without a break

16. not going well together; incompatible

17. a synonym for *boredom*

18. to block or hinder

WORDLY WISE 13

The word GAUNTLET appears in two common phrases: "to throw down the *gauntlet*," meaning to issue a challenge and "to take up the *gauntlet*," meaning to accept the challenge. Another meaning of the word occurs in the phrase "to run the *gauntlet*." Someone in this position is made to pass between two lines of people armed with clubs, with which they strike the person, hence the meaning of the word to undergo any gruelling ordeal or test. In this last context, the word is sometimes spelled *gantlet*.

HETERODOX means "opposed to the views generally held." Its antonym is *orthodox*, which means "conforming to the beliefs generally held." Both words are used particularly in reference to religious beliefs. *Heterodox* is formed from the Greek words *heteros* (other) and *doxa* (opinion); *orthodox* is formed from the Greek word *orthos* (right, true) and *doxa*.

MYRIAD is a general term that means "a large number." (A *myriad* of rumors circulated.) It comes from the Greek word *myrios* (countless), the plural of which, *myrioi*, meant "ten thousand."

Word List 14

BALEFUL	MALINGERER	TESTIMONY
DEMISE	OBESE	TONIC
EUPHORIA	PITHY	TOURNIQUET
FUTILE	SILO	TRACTABLE
HACKNEYED	SURREPTITIOUS	UNCOUTH
LATENT		

Look up the words above in your dictionary. Note that some of the words have more than one meaning. When you feel that you know *all* the meanings of *all* the words, go on to the exercise below.

EXERCISE 14A

From the four choices under each phrase or sentence, you are to mark the one that is closest in meaning to the word appearing in italics. When the same word appears more than once, you should note that it is being used in a different sense.

1. a *tractable* horse
   (a) retired from active work (b) difficult to manage (c) able to haul heavy loads (d) easily-managed

2. a sudden *euphoria*
   (a) feeling of detachment (b) feeling of despair (c) feeling of giddiness (d) feeling of well-being

3. a *surreptitious* move
   (a) clever (b) stealthy (c) sudden (d) baffling

4. a *latent* talent
   (a) hidden (b) fully-developed (c) useful (d) artistic

5. a *pithy* saying
   (a) trite and overused (b) suddenly popular (c) brief and meaningful (d) in Latin or Greek

6. the *pith* of a plant
   (a) hard outer layer of the stem (b) soft inner tissue of the stem (c) part that grows above ground (d) part that grows below ground

7. a *hackneyed* expression
   (a) striking (b) overused (c) strange (d) poetic

8. an *obese* person
    (a) obliging (b) fat (c) smart (d) proud

9. a person's *demise*
    (a) birth (b) death (c) property (d) character

10. the *demise* of an estate
    (a) extent (b) transfer (c) ownership (d) value

11. to recommend a *tonic*
    (a) minor operation (b) medicine that restores vitality (c) set of daily exercises (d) vacation spot in a healthful climate

12. a *baleful* look
    (a) full of hate (b) full of fear (c) full of love (d) full of despair

13. to apply a *tourniquet*
    (a) splint designed to hold a broken limb (b) cold compress designed to reduce fever (c) tight bandage designed to reduce bleeding (d) field dressing used to treat a wound

14. an *uncouth* person
    (a) untrustworthy (b) crude (c) fearless (d) cowardly

15. to hear the *testimony*
    (a) speech of welcome (b) appeal for help (c) statement made under oath (d) decision handed down by a judge

16. a *silo* on a farm
    (a) tower for storing water (b) tower for storing fodder (c) mill for grinding flour (d) van for transporting animals

17. accused of being a *malingerer*
    (a) person who complains constantly (b) person who habitually lies (c) person who betrays a trust (d) person who pretends to be ill

18. a *futile* attempt
    (a) successful (b) determined (c) useless (d) bold

Check your answers against the correct ones below. The answers are not in order; this is to prevent your eye from catching sight of the correct ones before you have had a chance to do the exercise on your own.

17d. 3b. 7b. 6b. 12a. 2d. 11b. 1d. 15c. 10b. 5c. 16b. 18c. 8b. 14b. 4a. 13c. 9b.

Go back to your dictionary and look up again those words for which you gave incorrect answers. Only after doing this should you go on to the next exercise.

EXERCISE 14B

Each word in Word List 14 is used four times in the sentences below; one of the sentences in each group uses the word incorrectly. You are to circle the letter that precedes that sentence. Do not circle more than one letter in any one group.

1. (a) The fact that the explosion could be heard fifteen miles away was vivid *testimony* to its force. (b) *Testimony* given before a grand jury is secret. (c) The fingerprints on the jewels were the *testimony* that convicted the thief. (d) The graceful bearing of these dancers is a *testimony* to their instructors.

2. (a) Her hand was bleeding so badly that we decided to apply a *tourniquet* to her arm. (b) Permanent damage may be caused if a *tourniquet* is kept in position for too long. (c) A *tourniquet* may be fashioned by wrapping a bandage around the limb and tightening it with a stick. (d) Our school won the interstate debating *tourniquet*.

3. (a) *Obese* persons are more likely to have heart attacks than slim persons. (b) The doctor told him to avoid red meat, butter, and other *obese* foods. (c) The best cure for *obesity* is exercise and a healthy diet. (d) Even for a pig, the sow was quite *obese*.

4. (a) Running can bring about a feeling of *euphoria*. (b) He deplored the use of such *euphoric* terms as "passed away" for "died." (c) The patient's mood alternates between *euphoria* and melancholy. (d) She was in such a *euphoric* mood that I assumed she had just received some good news.

5. (a) The horses eat *silo* during the winter. (b) The only buildings on the farm were a house, two barns, and a large *silo*. (c) A *silo* is an airtight cylindrical container, above or below ground, used for storing fodder. (d) Missiles are stored in underground *silos*, ready for instant firing.

6. (a) The villagers lived in deadly fear of the King's *baleful* temper (b) *Baleful* dark clouds massed on the horizon, threatening stormy weather. (c) Her stomach felt *baleful* from the green apples she had eaten. (d) The old man's *baleful* predictions of terrible disasters seemed about to come true.

7. (a) His sudden *demise* was a great shock to us all. (b) The *demise* of the newspaper was caused by a number of circumstances. (c) The falling tree struck him in the head, *demising* him instantly. (d) The house had been *demised* to her for a period of ten years under the terms of the lease.

8. (a) Gold, which can be beaten into leaf or drawn into wire, is one of the most *tractable* of metals. (b) The children are extremely *tractable* and obey orders without question. (c) She was nervous about riding and asked to be given a *tractable* horse. (d) Most planes have *tractable* landing gear to cut down wind resistance in flight.

9. (a) After failing so many times, he became *futile* and gave up. (b) They give up only when it seemed completely *futile* to continue. (c) After a *futile* discussion in which nothing was resolved, the meeting broke up. (d) She quickly saw the *futility* of trying to explain what she had hoped to accomplish.

10. (a) It is considered *uncouth* to speak with one's mouth full. (b) He felt *uncouth* in the presence of such refined gentlemen. (c) "I ain't got none o' them," he *uncouthed*. (d) She was so *uncouth* in her speech and style of dress that she made a bad impression.

11. (a) She looked extremely *hackneyed* after her long journey. (b) His speech was full of *hackneyed* phrases and stale jokes. (c) The movie's theme is the *hackneyed* one of the mysterious stranger who opposes evil. (d) The same *hackneyed* lines are heard over and over again in television westerns.

12. (a) The *latent* image in the photographic film is brought out by the developer. (b) Her teacher encouraged her to develop her *latent* talent. (c) The treasure was *latent* somewhere on the island, but we didn't know where to start digging for it. (d) The time between the contracting of a disease and the first sign of symptoms is called the *latency* period.

13. (a) A few of the men on sick call were genuinely ill, but most of them were *malingerers*. (b) Malaria is a *malingering* disease that may flare up again years after it has been contracted. (c) The teacher thought the student who had complained of a headache was *malingering*. (d) The doctor knew the names of those who were inclined to *malinger* and dealt firmly with them.

14. (a) This medicine will soon have you feeling *tonic* again. (b) The *tonic* effect of hot baths is well known. (c) He had been feeling rundown and was in need of a *tonic*. (d) The *tonic* air of the seaside soon put the color back in our cheeks.

15. (a) She writes in a *pithy* style that is a joy to read. (b) "I assumed command and defeated the enemy," the general said *pithily* when he was asked about the battle. (c) She expressed her idea with *pithy* and vividness. (d) The *pithy* substance from the reeds is removed, and the hollow tubes thus formed are used as blowpipes.

16. (a) The papers were removed *surreptitiously* from the office during the manager's absence. (b) The guard stepped into a patch of moonlight and enjoyed a *surreptitious* read through the newspaper. (c) She sidled up to me and *surreptitiously* slipped the package into my hand. (d) The authorities became *surreptitious* that the corporation was engaged in illegal activities.

EXERCISE 14C

Rewrite each of the sentences below, replacing the italicized word or phrase with a word from Word List 14 and writing the word in the form that fits the rest of the sentence. Use each word only once. Write your answers in the spaces provided.

1. The *person who was feigning illness in order to avoid working* soon saw that the attempt to fool the doctor was *vain and ineffectual.*

   . . . .

   . . . .

2. In his *statement given under oath*, the farmer declared that the *airtight tower used for storing fodder* had been damaged in the hurricane.

   . . . .

   . . . .

3. He gave me a *hateful and evil* look when I accused him of being *crude and ill-mannered.*

   . . . .

   . . . .

4. Her *death* could have been prevented had someone applied a *tightly twisted bandage to prevent bleeding.*

   . . . .

   . . . .

5. You may have an *as yet unrevealed* talent for painting.

   . . . .

   . . . .

6. This *medicine that restores strength and vitality* is recommended for people who are *extremely overweight*.

   . . . .

   . . . .

7. Her speech was quite *short and packed with meaning* although in places a few phrases were rather *overused.*

   . . . .

   . . . .

8. My horse was very *easy to manage* until someone, *stealthily and without being seen*, jabbed it with a stick.

   . . . .

   . . . .

9. What could be the cause of her *feeling of well-being*?

   . . . .

   . . . .

EXERCISE 14D

TOURNIQUET is derived from the French word *tourner* (to turn). Studies show that of the one thousand most frequently used words in the English language, over 30% are of French origin. Perhaps even more significant is the fact that over 60% are of Old English or Anglo-Saxon origin, with the remainder divided among Latin, Greek, and various other European and world languages. If we took all the words in modern English (there may be as many as a million), we would see a marked change in these figures with words of Latin origin accounting for over 40% of the total.

In a dictionary that gives word origins, look up each of the words in the sentence below. Under each word write the language from which it originated. Most of the following languages are represented at least once: German, Sanskrit, Spanish, Anglo-Saxon, Arabic, Dutch, Latin, Chinese, Tahitian, and French.

The	tattooed
. . . .	. . . .
buccaneer	casually
. . . .	. . . .
smoked	cigars
. . . .	. . . .
and	drank
. . . .	. . . .
lemon	tea
. . . .	. . . .
with	sugar
. . . .	. . . .
before	departing
. . . .	. . . .
for	his
. . . .	. . . .
yacht	with
. . . .	. . . .
the	plunder.
. . . .	. . . .

EXERCISE 14E

Write out, in the spaces provided, the words from Word List 14 for which a definition, synonym, or antonym is given on the next page. When you are asked to give a root or a prefix, you should refer back to the preceding exercise; the information you require will be found there. Make sure that each of your answers has the same number of letters as there are spaces. A definition followed by a number is a review word; the number gives the Word List from which it is taken.

If all the words are filled in correctly, the boxes running down the answer spaces will give you the first six words of a quotation from the works of the Roman philosopher Marcus Aurelius, who lived from A.D. 121 to 180. Marcus Aurelius ruled as Roman emperor from A.D. 161 until his death. His most famous book is *Meditations.* The quotation will be continued in Exercise 15E.

1. a synonym for *death*

2. a feeling of well-being

3. one who feigns illness to avoid a duty

4. an antonym for *refined*

5. easily-managed

6. a synonym for *stealthy*

7. brief and full of meaning

8. an airtight tower used for storing fodder

9. a tightly-twisted bandage used to stop bleeding

10. an antonym for *original*

11. vain; useless

12. strong and bold (13)

13. full of hate; evil

14. a medicine that restores health and vigor

15. to block or hinder (13)

16. a total lack of order (11)

17. profitable (12)

18. not yet revealed; hidden

19. evidence given solemnly, as under oath

20. an antonym for *thin*

WORDLY WISE 14

BALEFUL means "full of hate; evil" (a *baleful* look); don't confuse this word with *baneful*, which means "destructive; deadly" (a baneful influence).

A *hackney* was the horse-drawn forerunner of the modern taxicab; the horses used to pull these heavy carriages quickly became tired and worn out and were said to be HACKNEYED. The term later came to be applied to phrases or expressions that had become stale and worn out through overuse. ("She has a heart of gold" is a *hackneyed* expression.)

Word List 15

APTITUDE	IRONY	POROUS
ASTRAL	MISANTHROPE	PREVALENT
CONVERSANT	NOMINAL	SATURATE
DICTION	OMNISCIENT	SERE
ELLIPSIS	OSIER	USURY
HUMDRUM		

Look up the words above in your dictionary. Note that some of the words have more than one meaning. When you feel that you know *all* the meanings of *all* the words, go on to the exercise below.

EXERCISE 15A

From the four choices under each phrase or sentence, you are to mark the one that is closest in meaning to the word appearing in italics. When the same word appears more than once, you should note that it is being used in a different sense.

1. *astral* light
   (a) of the moon (b) of the stars (c) of the sun (d) invisible

2. *prevalent* diseases
   (a) incurable (b) extremely rare (c) preventable (d) widespread

3. undue use of *ellipsis*
   (a) words of many syllables (b) figures of speech (c) intentional omission of words (d) gestures accompanying words

4. *porous* materials
   (a) that do not combine chemically (b) that crumble easily (c) that can be poured easily (d) that allow fluids to pass through

5. her clear *diction*
   (a) view of someone or something (b) right to ownership (c) way of pronouncing words (d) understanding of a principle

6. his muddled *diction*
   (a) set of ideas (b) manner of expression (c) situation (d) attempt to improve matters

7. to *saturate* the clothes
   (a) fold (b) soak (c) choose (d) stain

8. a *saturated* space
   (a) fully enclosed (b) empty (c) open on all sides (d) completely filled

9. an *osier* chair
   (a) made of wrought iron (b) made of willow branches (c) leather-covered (d) stuffed with horsehair

10. *conversant* with it
    (a) in conversation (b) familiar (c) associated (d) encumbered

11. a lifelong *misanthrope*
    (a) person who hates people (b) person who tries to do good (c) person with outdated ideas (d) person in poor health

12. to become *sere*
    (a) wise (b) angry (c) tired (d) withered

13. the use of *irony*
    (a) remarks apparently opposite in meaning to their literal sense (b) words substituted for others considered unpleasant (c) overly polite and flowery language (d) comparisons between apparently dissimilar things

14. a *humdrum* life
    (a) long (b) short (c) monotonous (d) exciting

15. a *nominal* ruler
    (a) possessing popular support (b) possessing absolute power (c) elected by the people (d) in name only

16. a *nominal* sum
    (a) small (b) large (c) fixed (d) variable

17. an *omniscient* god
    (a) knowing all things (b) present everywhere (c) all-powerful (d) of the ancient world

18. an *aptitude* for something
    (a) appetite (b) ability (c) dislike (d) reason

19. accused of *usury*
    (a) practicing medicine without a license
    (b) lending money at excessive interest
    (c) giving in too easily to other people
    (d) spreading false and malicious gossip

Check your answers against the correct ones below. The answers are not in order; this is to prevent your eye from catching sight of the correct ones before you have had a chance to do the exercise on your own.

17a. 3c. 7b. 6b. 12d. 19b. 2d. 11a. 1b. 15d. 10b. 5c. 16a. 18b. 8d. 14c. 4d. 13a. 9b.

Go back to your dictionary and look up again those words for which you gave incorrect answers. Only after doing this should you go on to the next exercise.

EXERCISE 15B

Each word in Word List 15 is used four times in the sentences below; one of the sentences in each group uses the word incorrectly. You are to circle the letter that precedes that sentence. Do not circle more than one letter in any one group.

1. (a) The queen is merely a *nominal* ruler; actual power is exercised by the prime minister. (b) The registration number consisted of five *nominals,* the first three being 4, 7, and 9. (c) Nine tenths of this group are *nominally* Democrats, but less than a third actually vote. (d) The equipment was worth over a hundred dollars but was sold for the *nominal* sum of five dollars.

2. (a) "For Brutus is an honourable man; / So are they all, all honourable men," says Mark Antony *ironically* of the conspirators in **Julius Caesar.** (b) It is *ironical* that the things we want so badly in youth mean so little when we receive them later in life. (c) In debate she liked to *irony* her opponent into making false statements. (d) A writer with a gift for *irony* is able to express his case with subtlety and wit.

3. (a) After six months in Europe, she felt *saturated* with culture. (b) He loaded the van until it was *saturated* with the furniture. (c) She *saturated* the sponge with warm water and washed her face and neck. (d) Water continues to dissolve salt until it reaches its *saturation* point.

4. (a) Leather is a good material for shoes because it is light, flexible, and *porous.* (b) Water sinks below the surface immediately because the soil is so *porous.* (c) This *porous* material makes a good filter because it traps impurities while allowing the clear water to pass through. (d) She clasped her hands together in a *porous* attitude and began to pray.

5. (a) So *omniscient* is this poison that a single drop could kill hundreds of people. (b) The *omniscient* author tells us not only what the characters say but what they think and feel. (c) "I can't know everything that's going on," he protested. "I'm not *omniscient.*" (d) The fortune-teller's *omniscience* is presumed to extend to future as well as past events.

6. (a) The leaves, *sere* in the autumn sun, fall slowly—one by one. (b) The whole countryside grew *sere* as the fierce sun blazed down day after day. (c) The old butler, stooped and *sere* with age, opened the door to admit us. (d) You should *sere* the meat first to seal in the juices.

7. (a) Any of the willows whose twigs can be twisted into shape are referred to as *osiers.* (b) *Osier* baskets are strong, light, and attractive in appearance. (c) The long pliable branches of the *osier* are woven into various articles. (d) We watched the *osiers* weaving baskets out of long willow wands.

8. (a) The *prevalence* of burglaries in this area is worrying local residents. (b) When there is disagreement between us, his views are usually *prevalent* over mine. (c) The belief that the earth was flat was once *prevalent.* (d) Families with two cars are now *prevalent* where one-car families were once a rarity.

9. (a) The lending of money at reasonable rates is allowed, but *usury* is forbidden. (b) These people are *usurers* who charge as much interest as they can squeeze out of their victims. (c) The bank refused him a loan, so he went to a *usury* for one. (d) Such *usurious* rates of interest are to be condemned.

10. (a) He worked for forty years as a bank clerk, a life many would consider *humdrum*. (b) She *humdrummed* her way through life, content to remain in a little rut. (c) He found military life, with its parades, drills, and guard duties, a *humdrum* affair. (d) Field trips and audio-visual aids help to make school less *humdrum*.

11. (a) The *diction* employed by the artist in her later paintings differs from that in her earlier works. (b) She is taking speech lessons to improve her *diction*. (c) The *diction* of a serious essay is more formal than that of everyday speech. (d) Her *diction* is so poor that one cannot understand her half the time.

12. (a) An *ellipsis* in quoted material is usually indicated by a series of dots. (b) An example of *ellipsis* is "You coming?" for "Are you coming with us?" (c) *Ellipsis* is more common in everyday speech than in writing. (d) An *ellipsis* is a closed curve in the shape of an oval.

13. (a) Children with an *aptitude* for engineering should be encouraged to take science courses. (b) He has the right *aptitude* to his work and should do well. (c) She has an *aptitude* for telling people the truth without giving offense. (d) *Aptitude* tests are designed to predict a person's ability to learn particular skills.

14. (a) He *misanthroped* his way through life, despising man and all his works. (b) She denies being a *misanthrope* although she cannot name a single person she likes. (c) The fact that he avoids people is not proof of his *misanthropy*. (d) The cruelties that man practices against man make him a *misanthrope*.

15. (a) Are you *conversant* with the methods employed here? (b) Four or five *conversants* used to meet every morning for coffee. (c) Anyone *conversant* with other parts of the world must have found this little spot depressing. (d) Low-priced recordings make it possible for anyone to make himself *conversant* with the world's great music.

16. (a) Large telescopes reveal the existence of untold millions of *astral* bodies. (b) *Astral* light has different properties from the light reflected off the planets. (c) She gave an *astral* performance last night in her recital of operatic arias. (d) The radiations so far detected are believed to be *astral* in origin.

EXERCISE 15C

Rewrite each of the sentences below, replacing the italicized word or phrase with a word from Word List 15 and writing the word in the form that fits the rest of the sentence. Use each word only once. Write your answers in the spaces provided.

1. He doesn't claim to be *able to know everything*, but he is a scholar of great *natural ability and talent*.

. . . .

. . . .

2. Since the interest he charged you was *very small*, you cannot accuse him of *lending money at excessive rates of interest*.

. . . .

. . . .

3. I asked him what he thought of such *boring and monotonous* work; "I love it," he answered, *obviously meaning the exact opposite of what he had said.*

. . . .

. . . .

4. The years had not softened him, though he was *dried and wrinkled* with age, for he was still a *person with a deep hatred of mankind.*

....

....

5. Are you *familiar* with the methods used in making furniture from *the pliable branches of the willow?*

....

....

6. An *intentional omission of certain words* in quoted material is indicated by three dots.

....

....

7. These radiations are definitely *originating from the stars.*

....

....

8. The soil is *full of holes that allow the water to pass through* and therefore never gets *thoroughly soaked* by the rains.

....

....

9. I notice that carelessness in *the pronunciation of words* is becoming *more and more widespread* among young people.

....

....

EXERCISE 15D

From the Latin *dicere* (to say; to speak), we derive the root *dict*, which is found in a number of English words. DICTION, for example, is formed from this root plus the noun suffix *-ion.*

Complete the words below by filling in the appropriate form of the Latin root that means "say" or "speak." Prefixes and suffixes have been supplied. Write a brief definition of each word.

1. _____ APHONE

....

....

2. PRE _____

....

....

3. _____ IONARY

....

....

4. CONTRA _____

....

....

5. IN _____

....

....

6. _____ ATE

....

....

7. INTER _____

....

....

8. _____ ATOR

. . . .

. . . .

9. _____ UM

. . . .

. . . .

EXERCISE 15E

Write out, in the spaces provided, the words from Word List 15 for which a definition, synonym, or antonym is given below. When you are asked to give a root or a prefix, you should refer back to the preceding exercise; the information you require will be found there. Make sure that each of your answers has the same number of letters as there are spaces. A definition followed by a number is a review word; the number gives the Word List from which it is taken.

If all the words are filled in correctly, the boxes running down the answer spaces will continue the quotation begun earlier.

1. a person who hates mankind

2. a synonym for *widespread*

3. of or relating to the stars

4. an antonym for *exciting*

5. to criticize harshly (7)

6. allowing fluids or air to pass through

7. dry and withered

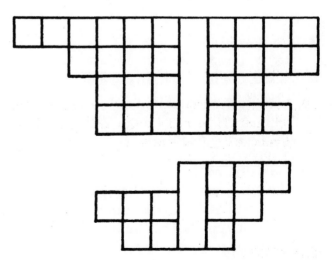

8. remarks with a literal meaning opposite from the intended meaning
9. manner of pronouncing words
10. the lending of money at excessive rates of interest

11. to soak thoroughly

12. a willow used for making baskets and furniture

13. in name only

14. facts from which conclusions can be drawn (7)

15. the intentional omission of a word or words

16. a Latin root meaning "speak"

17. having acquaintance, familiar

18. a rocky, picturesque cave (7)

19. a natural ability to learn

20. knowing all things

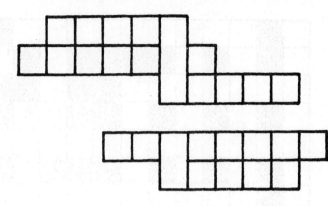
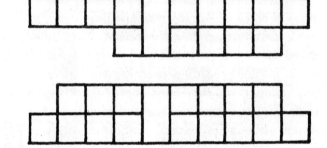

WORDLY WISE 15

ASTRAL and *stellar* both mean "of or relating to the stars"; *aster* is the Greek word for "star," and *stella* is the Latin word. Remember, however, that *aster* is also a Latin word because it was adopted by Latin as *astrum*. Note that *stellar* has wider application to stars of the entertainment world (a stellar cast).

SERE is a poetic term meaning "dried and withered" (the *sere* leaves of autumn). Note the spelling of its two homonyms *sear* (to burn the surface of) and *seer* (one who foresees the future; a prophet).

USURY is pronounced *YOO-zhu-ri*.

Across

2. made trite through overuse
8. something that is against the law
10. of or relating to the stars
11. in name only
14. a natural ability to learn
15. done secretly or stealthily
16. not going well together; inappropriate
19. one who hates and distrusts mankind
21. an airtight tower for storing fodder
24. to soak thoroughly
26. easily managed
27. a wild and uncontrolled merrymaking
28. manner of expression in words
30. following in order without a break
32. remark apparently opposite in meaning to its literal sense
34. to remove; to wipe out
37. the intentional omission of words
41. useless; vain
43. willow used to make various articles
44. a tightly twisted bandage used to prevent bleeding
45. differing from the accepted view
46. overweight; very fat
47. not sheltered; exposed; bare
48. shoddy and disreputable (6)
49. a gullible person from the country
50. to block or hinder

Down

1. knowing all things
2. dull, boring, and monotonous
3. familiar; having an acquaintance
4. a feeling of boredom or weariness
5. lasting or staying but a short time
6. one who pretends illness to avoid a duty
7. full of hate; evil
9. a feeling of great well-being
12. not yet revealed; hidden
13. allowing fluids and air to pass through
17. money lending at excessive rates of interest
18. of or relating to the sun
20. one who opposes the official view of his church (12)
22. to force out; to eject (4)
23. a protective leather or armored glove
25. a medicine that restores strength and energy
28. the death, especially of a person
29. a large number
30. willing to believe anything (6)
31. statements given under oath in court
33. widely accepted; widespread
35. to predict; to tell in advance
36. departing from what is usual or normal
38. dry and withered
39. bold and strong
40. brief and meaningful
42. crude; ill-mannered

93

Chapter Six

Word List 16

ACIDULOUS	IDOLATRY	PROLIFIC
ATTEST	IRRELEVANT	RECOMPENSE
DEVIOUS	LEACH	REGIMEN
ENSURE	MEDITATE	TITANIC
FALLIBLE	NONCOMMITTAL	WRAITH
GAUDY		

Look up the words above in your dictionary. Note that some of the words have more than one meaning. When you feel that you know *all* the meanings of *all* the words, go on to the exercise below.

EXERCISE 16A

From the four choices under each phrase or sentence, you are to mark one that is closest in meaning to the word appearing in italics. When the same word appears more than once, you should note that it is being used in a different sense.

1. *devious* methods
   (a) overly complicated (b) underhanded (c) straightforward (d) effective

2. a *devious* route
   (a) direct (b) roundabout (c) prearranged (d) alternate

3. a *noncommittal* reply
   (a) capable of being understood either way (b) giving no clear indication of attitude (c) indicating a refusal or denial (d) not given in writing

4. to *recompense* someone
   (a) speak favorably of (b) repay (c) accuse (d) raise to a higher position

5. on a *titanic* scale
   (a) very large (b) very small (c) variable (d) fixed

6. *prolific* creatures
   (a) no longer in existence (b) producing many offspring (c) long-lived (d) found all over the world

7. to see the *wraith*
   (a) ghost (b) puff of smoke (c) small poisonous snake (d) light

8. to be *fallible*
   (a) likely to err (b) doomed to die (c) willing to believe anything (d) quick to anger

9. to *meditate*
   (a) recover slowly (b) think quietly (c) receive medical aid (d) act as a go-between

10. to *meditate* revenge
    (a) plan (b) condemn (c) take (d) approve

11. a strict *regimen*
    (a) system of diet or exercise (b) military code of behavior (c) guard in a penitentiary (d) training during childhood

12. to *attest*
    (a) declare to be true (b) withhold one's opinion (c) express one's hostility (d) withdraw one's approval

13. *irrelevant* remarks
    (a) expressing disrespect (b) not related to the subject (c) uproariously funny (d) unintentionally funny

14. *gaudy* costumes
    (a) expensive and well cut (b) showy and cheap-looking (c) dirty and ragged (d) plain and simple

15. to condemn *idolatry*
    (a) worship of physical objects as gods (b) unwillingness to work (c) unrealistic attitudes (d) lack of respect for others

16. an *acidulous* tone of voice
(a) gentle (b) sharp (c) funny (d) grave

17. to *leach* the salts in a substance
(a) combine acids with (b) dissolve and wash away (c) determine the quantity of (d) break down

18. to *ensure* success
(a) have a strong desire for (b) feel contempt for (c) make certain of (d) be doubtful of

Check your answers against the correct ones below. The answers are not in order; this is to prevent your eye from catching sight of the correct ones before you have had a chance to do the exercise on your own.

15a. 4b. 8a. 7a. 17b. 12a. 18c. 6b. 1b. 10a. 11a. 2b. 5a. 13b. 14b. 16b. 3b. 9b.

Go back to your dictionary and look up again those words for which you gave incorrect answers. Only after doing this should you go on to the next exercise.

EXERCISE 16B

Each word in Word List 16 is used four times in the sentences below; one of the sentences in each group uses the word incorrectly. You are to circle the letter that precedes that sentence. Do not circle more than one letter in any one group.

1. (a) It cost sixty dollars extra to *ensure* the car against loss or damage. (b) The rules exist to *ensure* the safety of those working here. (c) Steps are being taken to *ensure* that there will be enough food for the winter. (d) Hard work is still the best way to *ensure* success.

2. (a) The liquid has an *acidulous* taste, like that of vinegar. (b) In an *acidulous* voice the teacher demanded to know why we were late. (c) The police *acidulously* followed up every clue in the robbery case. (d) The *acidulous* tone of her letter betrayed her indignation.

3. (a) The moderator dismissed my question as *irrelevant* and called for the next question. (b) The supplies I ordered are *irrelevant* and can be returned. (c) The story is marred by discussions on the nature of human beings and other *irrelevancies*. (d) The *irrelevance* of her remarks was obvious to all, so I refrained from comment.

4. (a) He was forty pounds overweight, so his doctor put him on a strict *regimen*. (b) Everybody at the health spa has a *regimen* carefully worked out to suit their needs. (c) I need to *regimen* my exercise habits. (d) The *regimen* she put herself on called for her to eat low-fat meals and take daily walks.

5. (a) Smoke *wraithed* upward from the dying ashes of the fire. (b) That was no *wraith* you saw but a swirl of fog in the gloom. (c) The mysterious *wraithlike* form seemed about to speak. (d) The old woman had lost so much weight that she seemed but a *wraith* of her former self.

6. (a) Did you receive any *recompense* for the work you did? (b) I *recompensed* the various amounts and arrived at a figure of eighty-seven dollars. (c) We were adequately *recompensed* for our efforts. (d) You will be *recompensed* for any losses you may suffer.

7. (a) Water is used to *leach* out the alkalis from wood ashes. (b) To bleed patients, doctors would place bloodsucking *leaches* against their skin. (c) The soil has been *leached* of its minerals by torrential rains. (d) Her happiness has *leached* out the bitterness that once was in her.

8. (a) She loves the *gaudy* splendor of the circus ring. (b) He was *gaudily* dressed in red, white, and blue for the July Fourth parade. (c) The children painted their faces in *gaudy* greens and yellows. (d) He gave the girls flashy pieces of *gaudy* he had bought at the dime store.

9. (a) Since humans by their very nature are *fallible*, it is possible that errors have crept into these results. (b) Admit your *fallibility* and concede that you could have made a mistake. (c) These results have been tested so carefully that it is absurd to suggest that they might be *fallible*. (d) The wall is extremely *fallible* and needs to be propped up.

10. (a) After beginning vaguely, she quickly got down to *prolifics*. (b) From his *prolific* mind have come many startling discoveries. (c) She is a *prolific* author with over fifty books to her credit. (d) Mice are extremely *prolific* since they breed several times a year.

11. (a) He was dressed in dull, *noncommittal* clothes. (b) He answered *noncommittally* when I asked him if he agreed with me. (c) Her greeting was friendly enough, but she remained *noncommittal* when I pressed her for an answer. (d) The people I spoke to were *noncommittal*, but they said I would be hearing from them soon.

12. (a) The people who worshiped the golden calf they had made practiced *idolatry*. (b) Her love for him is so strong that it verges on *idolatry*. (c) The people gradually lost their faith in God and grew more and more *idolatry*. (d) My cousin believes that those who worship false gods will be forgiven their *idolatry* if they truly repent.

13. (a) Her honor was *attested* to by all who knew her. (b) The Indianapolis 500 course severely *attests* both people and machines. (c) The genuineness of the painting was *attested* by several experts. (d) The speed with which they defeated the enemy *attested* to their superior skill.

14. (a) Much of the monks' day was taken up in prayer and *meditation*. (b) He *meditated* what steps to take to prevent a recurrence of the problem. (c) I found her sitting crosslegged on the floor *meditating*. (d) She offered to *mediate* the dispute that had broken out between the two groups.

15. (a) A *titanic* struggle was soon to break out that would split the nation. (b) The conversion to the metric system was conducted on a near-*titanic* scale. (c) Public meetings were banned and other *titanic* steps considered to end the wave of protests. (d) A hurricane of *titanic* force tossed the ship about as though it were a cork.

16. (a) This model used to come only in black, but now it comes in *devious* colors. (b) He was so *devious* in his dealings with others that I soon learned not to trust him. (c) We made our way along the *devious* path of a dried-up river bed. (d) I had had enough of her *deviousness* and demanded that she be frank with us.

EXERCISE 16C

Rewrite each of the sentences below, replacing the italicized word or phrase with a word from Word List 16 and writing the word in the form that fits the rest of the sentence. Use each word only once. Write your answers in the spaces provided.

1. The new method *makes certain* that the salts are *dissolved and washed* out of the ores.

   . . . .

   . . . .

2. I pressed him for a definite answer, but he was *unwilling to give a clear indication of his attitude*.

   . . . .

   . . . .

3. In *sour and acid* tones she condemned *the worship of physical objects as gods*.

   . . . .

   . . . .

4. She is *not straightforward* in her dealings with others and refused to say whether we would be *paid* for our work.

. . . .

. . . .

5. An *enormously powerful* storm is approaching the Florida coast.

. . . .

. . . .

6. As a writer, he is certainly *able to produce large numbers of books,* but he is just as likely *to make mistakes* as anyone else.

. . . .

. . . .

7. A *ghost*like figure sat in the corner, *thinking deeply* on the state of the world.

. . . .

. . . .

8. Are you willing to *swear to* the value of this *system of diet and exercise?*

. . . .

. . . .

9. The fact that his tie is *showy and lacking in taste* is *not to the point* since we are discussing his academic standing.

. . . .

. . . .

EXERCISE 16D

The word DEVIOUS is made up of the Latin prefix *de-* (off, from, away), discussed in Exercise 10D, and the Latin *via* (road). A *devious* route is one that leads away from the traveled road.

The prefix *de-* has two other meanings which are: "reversed" (when we *de*frost food, we *reverse* the freezing process) and "down" (to *de*cline an invitation is to turn it *down*).

In the space provided between the parentheses, write the meaning of each of the italicized prefixes. Write a brief definition of each word.

1. *de*rail   (   )

. . . .

. . . .

2. *de*molish   (   )

. . . .

. . . .

3. *de*spoiled   (   )

. . . .

. . . .

4. *de*press   (   )

. . . .

. . . .

5. *de*capitate   (   )

. . . .

. . . .

6. *de*code   (   )

. . . .

. . . .

. . . .

7. *de*relict ( )   9. *de*mote ( )

. . . .

. . . .

8. *de*scend ( )   10. *de*duct ( )

. . . .

. . . .

EXERCISE 16E

Write out, in the spaces provided, the words from Word List 16 for which a definition, synonym, or antonym is given below. When you are asked to give a root or a prefix, you should refer back to the preceding exercise; the information you require will be found there. Make sure that each of your answers has the same number of letters as there are spaces. A definition followed by a number is a review word; the number gives the Word List from which it is taken.

If all the words are filled in correctly, the boxes running down the answer spaces will continue the quotation begun earlier.

1. a synonym for *ghost*

2. a system of diet and exercise

3. to pay; to make up for

4. an antonym for *straightforward*

5. a death (14)

6. extremely fat (14)

7. sour or acid in taste or manner

8. liable to err

9. not to the point

10. a Latin prefix meaning "reversed"

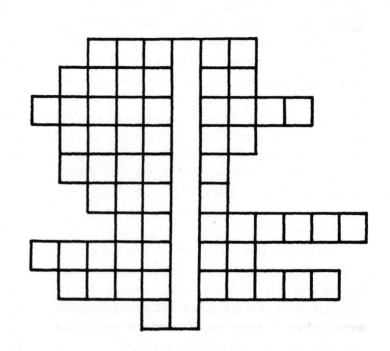

98

11. to remove; to wipe out (13)

12. the worship of physical objects as gods

13. to make certain

14. giving no clear indication of attitude

15. to dissolve and wash out

16. a synonym for *immense*

17. departing from what is usual or normal (13)

18. an antonym for *drab*

19. to declare to be true

20. a synonym for *ponder*

21. producing abundantly

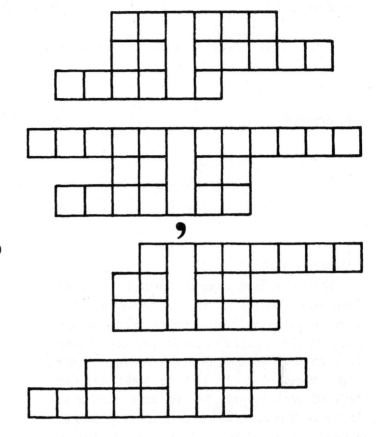

WORDLY WISE 16

ENSURE and *insure* both mean "to make certain; to make sure." *Insure*, in addition, has developed the specialized meaning "to guarantee against risk of loss or harm." (She *insured* her possessions to *ensure* that she would not be left penniless if her property were destroyed.) In this more restricted meaning the two terms are not interchangeable.

Don't confuse LEACH, which means "to dissolve and wash away" (to *leach* the minerals out of the soil), with its homonym *leech*, a blood-sucking worm used to bleed patients. A person who clings to another in hopes of getting something is called a *leech* through metaphorical extension of the term.

The origin of the word WRAITH is not known exactly and seems to have been introduced into English by the Scottish poet, Robert Burns. Originally a *wraith* was a person's ghost or apparition seen—perhaps as a warning or a means of protection —shortly or immediately *before* his death.

Word List 17

ADMINISTER	ENVOY	LUNAR
AQUILINE	GUILE	MIGRATORY
CLERIC	IMPEL	ORDNANCE
DEHYDRATE	**IMPOSTOR**	RESCIND
DELL	INVINCIBLE	VENEER
ELOCUTION		

Look up the words above in your dictionary. Note that some of the words have more than one meaning. When you feel that you know *all* the meanings of *all* the words, go on to the next exercise.

EXERCISE 17A

From the four choices under each phrase or sentence, you are to mark the one that is closest in meaning to the word appearing in italics. When the same word appears more than once, you should note that it is being used in a different sense.

1. *lunar* observations
   (a) of the planets (b) of the stars (c) of the sun (d) of the moon

2. to practice *elocution*
   (a) speaking in public (b) horseback riding (c) rifle shooting (d) acting without words

3. to *administer* the territory
   (a) divide up (b) incorporate into a larger state (c) give independence to (d) manage the affairs of

4. to *administer* medicine
   (a) ban the use of (b) treat disease with (c) take habitually (d) test the worth of

5. to *administer* the rebuke
   (a) deliver (b) receive (c) ignore (d) record

6. to *administer* the oath
   (a) solemnly take (b) act in accordance with (c) direct the taking of (d) learn the words of

7. to *dehydrate* milk
   (a) add water to (b) destroy the germs in (c) remove the fats from (d) remove the water from

8. to *rescind* the order
   (a) question (b) cancel (c) issue (d) obey

9. to *impel* someone to do something
   (a) force (b) ask (c) persuade (d) forbid

10. to *impel* the vehicle
    (a) seize (b) move (c) stop (d) license

11. a walnut *veneer*
    (a) glass-doored cabinet (b) finish that is painted on (c) thin surface layer (d) piece of furniture over 100 years old

12. to use *guile*
    (a) care (b) cunning (c) flattery (d) good judgment

13. *migratory* workers
    (a) organized into unions (b) moving from region to region (c) engaged in heavy industry (d) temporarily out of work

14. to meet in the *dell*
    (a) small private room (b) small city park (c) small country town (d) small secluded hollow

15. to be made an *envoy*
    (a) diplomatic officer ranked below ambassador (b) army officer ranked below a general (c) church official ranked below a bishop (d) law officer ranked below a judge

16. to act as an *envoy*
    (a) substitute (b) decoy (c) lookout (d) messenger

17. to be an *impostor*
    (a) person entrusted with a task (b) person who buys and sells wholesale (c) person claiming to be what he is not (d) person with a long criminal record

18. a young *cleric*
    (a) clergyman (b) lawyer (c) salesperson (d) office worker

19. an *aquiline* nose
    (a) pointed (b) snub (c) curved (d) flattened

20. in charge of *ordnance*
    (a) law enforcement (b) weapons of war (c) city government (d) hiring and firing workers

21. an *invincible* foe
    (a) treacherous (b) that cannot be defeated (c) that cannot be seen (d) that is present everywhere

Check your answers against the correct ones on the next page. The answers are not in order; this is to prevent your eye from catching sight of the correct ones before you have had a chance to do the exercise on your own.

7d. 1d. 5a. 15a. 17c. 10b. 20b. 19c. 4b. 12b. 21b. 13b. 3d. 8b. 18a. 11c. 9a. 6c. 2a. 16d. 14d.

Go back to your dictionary and look up again those words for which you gave incorrect answers. Only after doing this should you go on to the next exercise.

EXERCISE 17B

Each word in Word List 17 is used four times in the sentences below; one of the sentences in each group uses the word incorrectly. You are to circle the letter that precedes that sentence. Do not circle more than one letter in any one group.

1. (a) The city issued an *ordnance* against parking in the main street. (b) The enemy brought its heavy *ordnance* into position and began firing. (c) An *ordnance* officer is responsible for all military supplies. (d) The enemy had over ten thousand men but was lacking in *ordnance*.

2. (a) The woman claiming to be your long lost aunt is an *impostor*. (b) Her claim to the estate was denounced as a sham and an *imposture*. (c) He was able to *impostor* them into believing that he would inherit a large fortune. (d) Any person claiming to be me is an *impostor*.

3. (a) The cabinet was made of plywood covered with a teak *veneer*. (b) Drivers' licenses are *veneered* with plastic film to protect them. (c) The table is so skillfully *veneered* that it looks like solid walnut. (d) Under that *veneer* of friendliness is a cold heart.

4. (a) An appeal was made to the governor to *rescind* the harsh laws. (b) She refused to *rescind* the order despite the angry protest it aroused. (c) The government *rescinded* the treaty when it saw that the other country had no intention of abiding by it. (d) The money you paid will be *rescinded* from the amount you owe.

5. (a) Her *elocution* has improved greatly since she began taking voice lessons. (b) Her *elocution* teacher gave her some exercises designed to strengthen her voice. (c) He writes with such *elocution* that the reader is quite carried away. (d) Good *elocution* requires that you speak clearly and unhurriedly.

6. (a) My brother has been lifting weights, and now thinks himself *invincible* (b) The football team this season has proved itself *invincible*, winning all twelve games. (c) If this *invincible* weather continues, Saturday's game will have to be cancelled. (d) His *invincible* optimism sustained him through many dark moments.

7. (a) He was dressed in *clerical* garb, black suit, and reversed white collar. (b) We regret that due to a *cleric* error you were billed twice for the amount. (c) After taking his *clerical* vows, he settled down to a lifetime of service to his church. (d) The rabbi spoke informally to the *clerics* who were attending the religious conference.

8. (a) The children love to go to the *dell* and pick wild flowers. (b) We lay on our backs in the mossy *dell* and stared at the blue sky. (c) We used to picnic on the banks of a little stream that ran through the *dell*. (d) We could hear the *delling* of the church bells from a long way off.

9. (a) Her mind became *migratory* as she got older, so she moved into a retirement home. (b) *Migratory* workers travel across the country picking crops. (c) Wild geese are *migratory* birds and travel south as winter approaches. (d) These tribes *migrate* from region to region in search of food.

10. (a) *Dehydrated* foods can be reconstituted easily by adding water. (b) The fever *dehydrates* the patient's body, so he must have plenty to drink. (c) After the clothes are washed, they are *dehydrated* in the clothes dryer. (d) Fruit is *dehydrated* by being laid out in the sun.

11. (a) I *administered* first aid to the injured woman. (b) She didn't have the heart to *administer* a punishment to the mischievous boy. (c) She had charge of the entire department and proved herself an excellent *administer*. (d) A trust fund was set up to *administer* the inheritance.

12. (a) His blazing, deep-set eyes and *aquiline* nose gave him the fierce aspect of an eagle. (b) The *aquiline* profile of the Roman emperor appeared on all the coins. (c) She had the *aquiline* good looks of a Roman noblewoman. (d) His face was worn and *aquilined* with age.

13. (a) The *envoy* handled all diplomatic matters in the country. (b) The Secretary of State acted as an *envoy* for peace. (c) The president's special *envoy* to Japan arrived by plane this morning. (d) The message was *envoyed* to Washington without delay.

14. (a) We thought him an honest man and then realized he was nothing but a *guile*. (b) He *guilelessly* showed them where the rope was and was surprised when they used it to tie him up. (c) The people here are openhearted and friendly, completely lacking in *guile*. (d) This trusting old lady was no match for these *guileful* swindlers.

15. (a) She felt *impelled* to protest the treatment of animals at the farm. (b) What *impelled* him to do such a thing? (c) She felt a sudden *impel* to visit her old friend. (d) The submarine is *impelled* by two nuclear-powered engines.

16. (a) Jupiter is believed to have sixteen *lunars* circling it. (b) A *lunar* month is the period from new moon to new moon and lasts 29½ days. (c) A *lunar* eclipse occurs when the moon is obscured by the earth's shadow. (d) Pictures of the *lunar* landscape were transmitted from the moon by television cameras.

EXERCISE 17C

Rewrite each of the following sentences, replacing the italicized word or phrase with a word from Word List 17 and writing the word in the form that fits the rest of the sentence. Use each word only once. Write your answers in the spaces provided.

1. The new *weapons and ammunition of war* will make our army *impossible to defeat*.

   . . . .

   . . . .

2. She says she is a *diplomatic officer just below the rank of ambassador*, but she may be a *person who is not what she says she is*.

   . . . .

   . . . .

3. Exploration of the *moon's* surface still yields information.

   . . . .

   . . . .

4. The young man with the *hooked or curved* nose is studying *the art of speaking in public*.

   . . . .

   . . . .

5. This machine *removes all the moisture from the food*.

   . . . .

   . . . .

6. The *clergyman* who is most senior in rank *directs the taking of* the oath of office.

   . . . .

   . . . .

7. The birds that nest in this *small secluded hollow* are *of a kind that moves from region to region* and will soon fly south.

. . . .

. . . .

8. Under that *thin surface layer* of friendliness is a person of infinite *cunning and deceitfulness*.

. . . .

. . . .

9. She felt *driven* to *do away with* certain privileges.

. . . .

. . . .

EXERCISE 17D

Many common English nouns are of Anglo-Saxon origin but derive their adjectival forms from Latin. Our word *moon*, for example, comes from the Anglo-Saxon *mona*; however, our adjective meaning "of or relating to the moon" is LUNAR, from the Latin word *luna* for "moon."

Here are ten Latin words that form the roots of English adjectives:

stella	(star)
auris	(ear)
ferrum	(iron)
sol	(sun)
arbor	(tree)
canis	(dog)
felis	(cat)
terra	(earth)
equus	(horse)
dent	(tooth)

Using these words to form roots, construct adjectives to fit the following definitions. Check your answers in a dictionary for spelling and accuracy.

1. of or relating to cats

. . . .

2. of or relating to trees

. . . .

3. of or relating to the stars

. . . .

4. of or relating to dogs

. . . .

5. of or relating to the earth

. . . .

6. of or relating to the teeth

. . . .

7. of or relating to the sun

. . . .

8. of or relating to horses

. . . .

9. of or relating to iron

. . . .

10. of or relating to the ear

. . . .

EXERCISE 17E

Write out, in the spaces provided, the words from Word List 17 for which a definition, synonym, or antonym is given on the next page. When you are asked to give a root or a prefix, you should refer back to the preceding exercise; the information you require will be found there. Make sure that each of your answers has the same number of letters as there are spaces. A definition followed by a number is a review word; the number gives the Word List from which it is taken.

If all the words are filled in correctly, the

boxes running down the answer spaces will continue the quotation begun earlier.

1. moving from one region to another

2. manner of speaking in public

3. to remove moisture from; to dry out

4. following a winding or roundabout path (16)

5. to manage the affairs of

6. a synonym for *cunning*

7. curved like an eagle's beak

8. one who is not what he pretends to be

9. to force or urge

10. a synonym for *messenger*

11. to declare to be true (16)

12. an antonym for *grant*

13. a synonym for *priest*

14. liable to err (16)

15. a small, secluded hollow

16. a thin surface layer, usually of costly wood

17. of or relating to the moon

18. a synonym for *unconquerable*

19. weapons, ammunition, and other military supplies

WORDLY WISE 17

Don't confuse ORDNANCE, the term for guns, ammunition, and other military supplies, with *ordinance*, the term for a law or statute passed by a city or local government.

Word List 18

ADVENT	ILLITERATE	PRONE
APPALLED	LATERAL	RANGY
CRAVEN	LISSOME	SANCTUM
DILATE	ODOMETER	STENOGRAPHER
ETHEREAL	PENANCE	WRY
EXEMPLIFY	PEWTER	

Look up the words above in your dictionary. Note that some of the words have more than one meaning. When you feel that you know *all* the meanings of *all* the words, go on to the exercise below.

EXERCISE 18A

From the four choices under each phrase or sentence, you are to mark the one that is closest in meaning to the word appearing in italics. When the same word appears more than once, you should note that it is being used in a different sense.

1. a plate made of *pewter*
   (a) carved and polished wood (b) steel coated with silver (c) a tin and lead mixture (d) baked and glazed clay

2. a skilled *stenographer*
   (a) print maker (b) shorthand typist (c) script-writer (d) book illustrator

3. *ethereal* beauty
   (a) exotic (b) delicate (c) flawed (d) feminine

4. *ethereal* forms
   (a) constantly changing (b) present everywhere (c) light and airy (d) firm and solid

5. to *dilate* on the subject
   (a) remain silent (b) speak or write at length (c) forbid all discussion (d) throw light

6. to *dilate*
   (a) keep changing (b) grow larger (c) grow smaller (d) stay the same

7. a *craven* enemy
   (a) deadly (b) cowardly (c) confident (d) invincible

8. a *lateral* pass
   (a) forward (b) sideways (c) pretended (d) backward

9. a person's *sanctum*
   (a) right to trial by jury (b) place safe from intrusion (c) belief in God (d) right to worship

10. a religious *sanctum*
    (a) sacred place (b) sacred vow (c) sacred object (d) sacred picture

11. a *prone* position
    (a) lying face up (b) doubled up (c) lying face down (d) upright

12. *prone* to err
    (a) impossible (b) tending (c) certain (d) afraid

13. a lengthy *penance*
    (a) period of time served in prison (b) punishment for one's sins (c) talk on a religious subject (d) period of probation in a monastery

14. a *wry* smile
    (a) warmly affectionate (b) grimly or ironically humorous (c) nervously welcoming (d) coldly correct

15. a *rangy* youth
    (a) slow and dull-witted (b) slim and long-legged (c) short and dark-haired (d) quick and intelligent

16. a *lissome* child
    (a) young and inexperienced (b) tall and ungainly (c) supple and graceful (d) intelligent and kind

17. to *exemplify* virtue
    (a) try to encourage (b) be totally lacking in (c) be an example of (d) speak mockingly of

18. to be *illiterate*
    (a) in poor health (b) unable to read or write (c) abandoned by one's parents (d) a good writer.

19. the *advent* of winter
(a) shortest day (b) memory (c) coming (d) end

20. the four Sundays in *Advent*
(a) the period preceding Easter (b) the period preceding Christmas (c) the period following Easter (d) the period following Christmas

21. fitted with an *odometer*
(a) instrument for measuring height climbed
(b) instrument for measuring distance traveled
(c) instrument for recording the greatest speed
(d) instrument for measuring engine revolutions

22. to be *appalled*
(a) criticized (b) appointed (c) dismissed (d) horrified

Check your answers against the correct ones below. The answers are not in order; this is to prevent your eye from catching sight of the correct ones before you have had a chance to do the exercise on your own.

7b. 1c. 5b. 15b. 17c. 10a. 20b. 19c. 4c. 12b. 21b. 13b. 3b. 8b. 18b. 11c. 14b. 9b. 22d. 6b. 2b. 16c.

Go back to your dictionary and look up again those words for which you gave incorrect answers. Only after doing this should you go on to the next exercise.

EXERCISE 18B

Each word in Word List 18 is used four times in the following sentences; one of the sentences in each group uses the work incorrectly. You are to circle the letter that precedes that sentence. Do not circle more than one letter in any one group.

1. (a) The *advent* of the election was marked by more and more speeches from the politicians. (b) During *Advent,* which begins four Sundays before Christmas, Christians are expected to prepare themselves for that holy day. (c) Not once did he *advent* to the real reason for his visit. (d) The *advent* of spring is heralded by the appearance of the swallow.

2. (a) The dancers are tall and *lissome* and perform with incredible grace. (b) The lion yawned and *lissomed* its limbs in the warm sunshine. (c) We were fascinated by the *lissome* movements of the panther. (d) She moved with the *lissome* grace of a cat.

3. (a) Fugitives were once able to find *sanctum* in churches or other holy places. (b) The sacred objects of the religion are kept in the inner *sanctum* of the temple. (c) The editor's *sanctum* is a room to which she can retire without being disturbed. (d) The *sanctum* sanctorum, or holy of holies, is the innermost chamber of a Jewish temple.

4. (a) When Mark Antony says, "Lend me your ears," he does not mean it *laterally.* (b) A *lateral* pass in football is one to the player's left or right. (c) The branches grow out *laterally* from the trunk. (d) The upright columns support the *lateral* beams of the house.

5. (a) Music, so *ethereal* it seemed to come from heaven, floated through the trees. (b) The bride, *ethereal* in white lace, posed happily for photos. (c) She was *ethereal* with hunger when she was rescued because she had not eaten for ten days. (d) Liberty is not an *ethereal* thing but is always related to specific and present situations.

6. (a) When the pilot saw the *odometer* register 120,000 feet, he knew that he had broken the world's altitude record. (b) The car's *odometer* had been turned back to 5,000 miles. (c) Some cars have trip *odometers* that register distances up to 999.9 miles. (d) When this *odometer* reaches 99,999 miles, it will return to zero.

7. (a) By the end of four weeks of classes, many of the *illiterate* people could write their names and read simple stories. (b) She *illiterated* all traces of what she had done. (c) The government's compulsory education plan is intended to wipe out *illiteracy.* (d) He is a musical *illiterate* and can't tell the difference between Beethoven and country music.

8. (a) The horses are big-boned, *rangy* animals, able to gallop at high speeds. (b) A *rangy* cowboy swung his legs over his horse and galloped off. (c) She squinted *rangily* at me when I called out her name. (d) He is a *rangy* youth, but he'll fill out as he gets older.

9. (a) She had a piece of cheese with *wry* bread for her lunch. (b) She smiled *wryly* to herself as she accepted their congratulations. (c) The *wry* humor of his speech delighted everyone. (d) She made a *wry* face when she tasted the drink.

10. (a) With proper training, they will be less *prone* to make mistakes. (b) Some people are accident-*prone* and cannot help making mistakes. (c) The dancers assumed *prone* positons and began their recital. (d) She stood upright, her feet planted *prone* on the ground.

11. (a) The pupils of our eyes *dilate* in poor light and contract in strong light. (b) The patient's heart became greatly enlarged, although the cause of the *dilation* is not known. (c) The author *dilates* on the theme of the son searching for the father. (d) The wine is *dilated* with water before it is served.

12. (a) A *stenographic* record was made of the witness's testimony. (b) The message was immediately *stenographed* to all parts of the world. (c) A skilled *stenographer* can take down over two hundred words a minute. (d) At the end of the course in *stenography*, you should be able to take shorthand at about 120 words per minute.

13. (a) The sight of the injured children *appalled* him. (b) Her face *appalled* when she heard the news. (c) An *appalling* number of people do not exercise their right to vote. (d) I was *appalled* when I heard how badly you had been treated.

14. (a) She *exemplified* the virtues of the frontierswoman: resourcefulness and generosity. (b) Her work *exemplifies* all that is best in modern sculpture. (c) Because he was sick, he was *exemplified* from taking the test that day (d) Leonardo da Vinci was the *exemplar* of a Renaissance person.

15. (a) The Catholic Church requires its members to do *penance* for sins. (b) He was required to do volunteer work as *penance* for breaking the law. (c) The *penance* for armed robbery is ten years' imprisonment. (d) The priest imposes a *penance* after hearing the confession.

16. (a) *Pewter* is a mixture of tin and lead. (b) She had a *pewter* tankard with a glass bottom. (c) The antique store has a large assortment of *pewter* at reasonable prices. (d) A large glass *pewter* stood on the library table.

17. (a) They had come to *craven* the pardon of their lord and master. (b) He made the logical, if *craven*, suggestion that the beseiged fort surrender. (c) He feared his sister would be *craven*, but she proved more brave than he. (d) "I am no *craven*, sir, because I refuse to duel with you," said the young cavalier.

EXERCISE 18C

Rewrite each of the following sentences, replacing the italicized word or phrase with a word from Word List 18 and writing the word in the form that fits the rest of the sentence. Use each word only once. Write your answers in the spaces provided.

1. I was *filled with dismay* when I found out that the *instrument that records distance traveled* in the car had been turned back a few thousand miles.

. . . .

. . . .

2. The plate is made of *a mixture of tin and another metal such as lead, brass, or copper.*

....

....

3. Until the *coming* of printing, most people in the world were *unable to read or write.*

....

....

4. I need a *person skilled in shorthand* to help me with these letters.

....

....

5. These honor-roll students, captains of the soccer and basketball teams, *are an example of all that is best in our school.*

....

....

6. The music, played by *supple and graceful* violinists, was so *delicately light and airy* that it seemed to come from heaven.

....

....

7. He's a *slim, long-legged* man, and he smiled *with an humorous twist to his mouth* when I asked him how tall he was.

....

....

8. I saw the pupils of his eyes *grow large* with fear, and I knew then what a *cowardly and fainthearted* fellow he was.

....

....

9. They lay *face down* on the floor with their arms extended *straight out from their sides.*

....

....

10. The *punishment imposed by the priest* for anyone unlawfully entering the *most sacred place* of the temple was a severe one.

....

....

EXERCISE 18D

The word STENOGRAPHER is made up of roots derived from two Greek words, *stenos* (little, narrow) and *graphein* (to write). Here are eight other Greek words:

phos	(light)
kardia	(heart)
phone	(sound)
lithos	(stone)
tele	(far off)
bios	(life)
logos	(word, study of)
poly	(many)

By combining the Greek root *graph* (where necessary) with roots derived from the words above, construct words to fit the following definitions. Note that the Greek "k" often changes to "c" in English. Check each word in your dictionary for spelling and accuracy.

1. an instrument that reproduces sound from tracings made on flat discs

....

2. described in vivid and realistic detail

....

3. an instrument that records changes in electric potential produced by contractions of the heart

. . . .

4. an account of a person's life

. . . .

5. an instrument for recording tracings of several different pulsations simultaneously; a lie detector

. . . .

6. the craft of printing from a stone or plate, parts of which have been treated to repel ink

. . . .

7. a diagram or chart that shows changes taking place

. . . .

8. a picture reproduced on light-sensitive film or paper

. . . .

9. the art of reading character from handwriting

. . . .

10. an apparatus for sending messages by means of radio waves or by electric impulses sent through a wire

. . . .

EXERCISE 18E

Write out, in the spaces provided, the words from Word List 18 for which a definition, synonym, or antonym is given on the next page. When you are asked to give a root or a prefix, you should refer back to the preceding exercise; the information you require will be found there. Make sure that each of your answers has the same number of letters as there are spaces. A definition followed by a number is a review word; the number gives the Word List from which it is taken.

If all the words are filled in correctly, the boxes running down the answer spaces will continue the quotation begun earlier.

1. a synonym for *horrified*

2. a shorthand typist

3. supple and graceful

4. an alloy of tin with lead, brass or copper

5. an antonym for *solid*

6. with a humorous twist

7. producing abundantly (16)

8. lying in a face-down position

9. a Greek root meaning "write"

10. to be an example of

11. punishment accepted for wrongdoing

12. a sacred place

13. a synonym for *coming*

14. a device for measuring distance traveled

15. of, at, from or toward the sides

16. an antonym for *contract*

17. unable to read or write

18. slim and long-legged

19. curved like an eagle's beak (17)

20. a synonym for *cowardly*

WORDLY WISE 18

LISSOME is sometimes written *lissom*; both spellings are correct.

Note the different spelling of WRY and its homonym *rye*, the name of a cereal grain (rye bread). *Wry* can be used in various different contexts, all of which essentially mean "twisted." (She made a *wry* face after sipping the drink.)

When *wry* refers to a smile, it is a twisted expression or grimace to express irony or mockery. *Wry* humor is that which is marked by a clever twist, often with a hint of irony. Another interesting related word is *awry* (a, "on" the *wry*), meaning "twisted toward one side" or "askew." (His necktie was all *awry*.)

Across

1. one claiming to be what he is not
7. resembling an eagle's beak; curved
10. to be an example of
12. a thin surface layer, as of costly wood
14. lying in a face-down position
16. weapons and ammunition of war
17. giving no clear indication of attitude
18. to dissolve and wash out
19. sour or acid in taste or manner
22. a very wise old person (4)
23. following a winding, roundabout path
24. a messenger
27. to remove all water from; to dry out
30. manner of speaking publicly
32. not to the point
33. to repay; to make up for
35. deceitfulness; cunning
36. a ghost or apparition
38. a clergyman
40. an alloy of tin and lead
42. to declare to be true
44. of, at, toward or from the side
46. a two-wheeled, horse-drawn carriage (3)
50. one who celebrates noisily (5)
51. unable to read or write
52. filled with dismay; horrified
53. slim and long-legged

Down

1. that cannot be defeated
2. punishment accepted for wrongdoing
3. a person skilled in shorthand
4. to do away with; to cancel
5. to think quietly and deeply
6. to encircle as with a belt (2)
8. to drive or move forward
9. the worship of physical objects as gods
11. producing in abundance
13. to make certain
15. light and airy; delicate
20. supple and graceful
21. a place safe from intrusion
25. an instrument for measuring distance traveled
26. to manage the affairs of
28. to become wider or larger
29. a coming or arriving
31. moving from one region to another
34. liable to err
36. twisted
37. of great size, strength or power
39. a system of diet and exercise
41. cowardly; fainthearted
43. to spend as little as possible (9)
45. of or relating to the moon
47. showy and cheap-looking
48. a small, secluded hollow
49. to make one's way; to travel leisurely (2)

Chapter Seven

Word List 19

ABSTINENCE	FUROR	PRATE
BENEVOLENT	GLEAN	SCRIBE
BUFFOON	MASSACRE	TABOO
CHICANERY	MINIMIZE	TACIT
DENIZEN	PAPYRUS	VOID

Look up the words above in your dictionary. Note that some of the words have more than one meaning. When you feel that you know *all* the meanings of *all* the words, go on to the exercise below.

EXERCISE 19A

From the four choices under each phrase or sentence, you are to mark the one that is closest in meaning to the word appearing in italics. When the same word appears more than once, you should note that it is being used in a different sense.

1. to *glean* the facts
   (a) examine (b) interpret (c) disprove (d) gather

2. a sudden *furor*
   (a) attack (b) uproar (c) silence (d) change

3. a *tacit* agreement
   (a) verbal (b) unspoken (c) written (d) broken

4. a *benevolent* person
   (a) kindly (b) wicked (c) old (d) wise

5. The agreement is *void*.
   (a) in effect (b) without legal force (c) legally binding (d) not renewable

6. a huge *void*
   (a) waste (b) popular demand (c) volume (d) empty space

7. to *prate* of freedom
   (a) chatter foolishly (b) sing the praises (c) undertake the defense (d) bring about the loss

8. a terrible *massacre*
   (a) error in judgment (b) storm causing much damage (c) wound inflicted accidentally (d) killing of many people

9. to *minimize* the danger
   (a) reduce (b) estimate (c) exaggerate (d) ignore

10. to *minimize* someone's efforts
    (a) reward (b) understate (c) encourage (d) discourage

11. to write on *papyrus*
    (a) the prepared bark of birch trees (b) the prepared hide of young goats (c) soft clay tablets subsequently baked (d) paper made from stems of reeds, used for writing material in ancient Egypt

12. a *denizen* of the region
    (a) crude map (b) ruler (c) characteristic (d) inhabitant

13. a medieval *scribe*
    (a) book of prayer (b) soldier of the lowest rank (c) copier of· manuscripts (d) encirclement of a fortified place

14. a newspaper *scribe*
    (a) writer (b) column (c) headline (d) news story

15. to be a *buffoon*
    (a) person of extreme old age (b) person who acts the fool (c) person who acts as a guard (d) person who is unhappy

16. to suspect *chicanery*
    (a) trickery (b) murder (c) nothing (d) treason

17. total *abstinence*
    (a) recall of events of the past (b) inability to move the muscles (c) freedom to do as one pleases (d) doing without certain things

18. Dancing is *taboo*.
    (a) encouraged   (b) allowed   (c) discouraged
    (d) forbidden

Check your answers against the correct ones below. The answers are not in order; this is to prevent your eye from catching sight of the correct ones before you have had a chance to do the exercise on your own.

5b. 1d. 7a. 15b. 17d. 10b. 3b. 13c. 12d. 4a. 8d. 18d. 11d. 14a. 9a. 16a. 2b. 6d.

Go back to your dictionary and look up again those words for which you gave incorrect answers. Only after doing this should you go on to the next exercise.

EXERCISE 19B

Each word in Word List 19 is used four times in the sentences below; one of the sentences in each group uses the word incorrectly. You are to circle the letter that precedes that sentence. Do not circle more than one letter in any one group.

1. (a) Only by holding a public inquiry can we ensure that there is no *chicanery*. (b) The newspaper planned to expose the *chicaneries* of those who had abused their positions of trust. (c) About an ounce of *chicanery* is added to the coffee to make it go further. (d) He brought off his deception so cleverly that no *chicanery* was suspected.

2. (a) The boat was *buffooned* from side to side in the strong wind. (b) We soon tired of his *buffoonery* and decided to leave. (c) Some *buffoon* at the party grabbed a tablecloth and pretended to be a bullfighter. (d) I felt like a *buffoon* when I stood up to speak and found I had forgotten my speech.

3. (a) Proper precautions will *minimize* the risk of fire. (b) By exercising regularly she was able to *minimize* ten pounds in two months. (c) He was prone to *minimize* the importance of his actions. (d) Continued friendly relations between the two countries

have *minimized* the problems they once had with each other.

4. (a) The contract is *void* unless it is signed in the presence of two witnesses. (b) Her sudden death has left a *void* that nothing can fill. (c) The spaceship left the friendly surface of the planet and blasted off into the *void*. (d) To *void* any dispute, make sure that everyone understands the conditions.

5. (a) I have *gleaned* these figures over and over and can find no error in them. (b) She had *gleaned* all the information she was likely to from the witnesses. (c) Many useful ideas can be *gleaned* by browsing through this book. (d) After the reapers are finished, others go to the fields to *glean* the grain that has been missed.

6. (a) The *taboos* that govern behavior are so strong that no one dares break them. (b) His rapid hands beat out a *taboo* on the drum. (c) Mentioning the name of a dead person is *taboo* among these islanders. (d) In the nineteenth century there were rigid *taboos* against women going out to work.

7. (a) The golden eagle is king of the winged *denizens* of the air. (b) The *denizens* of our large cities are accustomed to noise and dirty air. (c) The giant squid, that most terrible of all the *denizens* of the deep, grows to enormous size. (d) The actors *denizen* themselves in medieval clothing.

8. (a) The manuscript had been translated from *Papyrus* into English. (b) *Papyrus* documents may be seen in most museums. (c) *Papyrus* was used as a writing material from about 400 B.C. to about A.D. 400. (d) The ancient Egyptians used strips of pith from the *papyrus* plant to make writing material.

9. (a) Let us not *prate* of victory until the game is won. (b) Ignore these *prating* fools with their idle chatter. (c) The horses *prated* around the ring, their hoofs lifted high with every

step. (d) I stared off into the distance as he *prated* on about his success in the business world.

10. (a) These practices enjoy the *tacit* support of the authorities. (b) The fact that she voiced no objection was taken as *tacit* approval of their plans. (c) The guard dog growled softly, a *tacit* warning to us not to go further. (d) "When I need your advice, I'll ask for it," she said *tacitly*.

11. (a) More and more people think drinking is harmful and practice total *abstinence*. (b) *Abstinence* from meat, strong drink, and cigarettes was her recipe for long life. (c) He was once a heavy drinker but has been *abstinent* for over five years. (d) He *abstinently* refused to answer the question.

12. (a) She worked as a *scribe* for one of the local newspapers. (b) The "*scribes* and Pharisees" mentioned in the Bible were the teachers and interpreters of Jewish law and those who strictly obeyed the laws. (c) He *scribed* something on the horizon that looked like a sail. (d) In the days before printing, books were hand written by *scribes*.

13. (a) Some people see meat-eating as a *massacre* of animals. (b) The *massacre* of General Custer's men at Little Big Horn occurred in 1876. (c) The driver and passengers were unhurt in the accident, but the car was badly *massacred*. (d) The visitors *massacred* the home team: the score was 57–0.

14. (a) She was feeling *benevolent* and contributed a thousand dollars to the fund-raising drive. (b) I admired the *benevolent* cut of his clothes and his easygoing manner. (c) Smiling *benevolently*, he gave each child a pat on the head and a dollar. (d) She showed her *benevolence* by agreeing to pay the boy's fine and find him a job.

15. (a) The *furor* created by her controversial book is only just beginning to die down. (b) Adolph Hitler proclaimed himself *Furor* of Germany in 1933. (c) In a *furor* of rage and terror, he hurled himself at his tormenter. (d) The threatened devaluation of the dollar created quite a *furor* on the stock market.

EXERCISE 19C

Rewrite each of the sentences below, replacing the italicized word or phrase with a word from Word List 19 and writing the word in the form that fits the rest of the sentence. Use each word only once. Write your answers in the spaces provided.

1. Alcohol is *strictly forbidden* in their family because they are firm believers in *never touching strong drink*.

   . . . .

   . . . .

2. She agreed *without actually saying anything* to what we were planning.

   . . . .

   . . . .

3. I thought of him simply as a *person who loves to play the fool* and never for a moment suspected him of *deceit and trickery*.

   . . . .

   . . . .

4. The *person whose job it was to copy manuscripts* wrote on sheets of *writing material made from pressed strips of the pith from certain Egyptian reeds.*

   . . . .

   . . . .

5. The *inhabitants* of the island avoided a *vio-*

lent and bloody mass killing by negotiating peacefully.

. . . .

. . . .

6. I was able to *gather with some difficulty* the facts concerning yesterday's *uproar* in the gym.

. . . .

. . . .

7. The death of that *kind and good-hearted* woman has left an *empty space* in all our lives.

. . . .

. . . .

8. He *chattered foolishly* of his own part in the affair and tried to *reduce the importance of our role*.

. . . .

. . . .

EXERCISE 19D

The Latin *scribere* (to write) gives us our word SCRIBE, a person who copied manuscripts before the advent of printing. From this Latin word is derived the root *scrib* or *script*, found in a number of English words.

By combining the appropriate form of this root with the following prefixes and suffixes, construct words to complete the following sentences. Note that in one case the root is combined with another Latin root *manu* (hand).

Prefixes: *circum-, con-, de-, in-, pre-, trans-, pro-*
Suffixes: *-ble, -ed, -ion, -ure*

1. She reads a passage from Holy. . . . . every morning.

2. After taking down the report in shorthand, he will . . . . his notes.

3. Please . . . . in your own words what happened.

4. There was a lengthy . . . . carved on the tombstone.

5. A circle that . . . . a pentagon touches it at all five corners.

6. The government plans to . . . . all able-bodied men into the army.

7. Travel to these countries is . . . . by law.

8. The pharmacist will make up the doctor's . . . .

9. Why did you give the baby a pencil and let him . . . . in my new notebook?

10. I delivered the . . . . of my new novel to the publisher yesterday.

EXERCISE 19E

Write out, in the spaces provided, the words from Word List 19 for which a definition, synonym, or antonym is given on the next page. When you are asked to give a root or a prefix, you should refer back to the preceding exercise; the information you require will be found there. Make sure that each of your answers has the same number of letters as there are spaces. A definition followed by a number is a review word; the number gives the Word List from which it is taken.

If all the words are filled in correctly, the boxes running down the answer spaces will conclude the quotation begun in Exercise 14E.

1. a small, secluded hollow (17)

2. one who copied manuscripts, in the days before printing

3. an antonym for *malevolent*

4. supple and graceful (18)

5. a voluntary self-denial of certain things

6. a synonym for *unspoken*

7. of or relating to the moon (17)

8. to chatter foolishly

9. a Latin root meaning "write"

10. a violent and mass killing

11. a synonym for *reduce*

12. a synonym for *inhabitant*

13. a synonym for *trickery*

14. one who plays the fool

15. to grow larger or wider (18)

16. to gather with difficulty

17. an antonym for *allowed*

18. writing material in the ancient times

19. slim and long-legged (18)

20. an empty space

21. a synonym for *uproar*

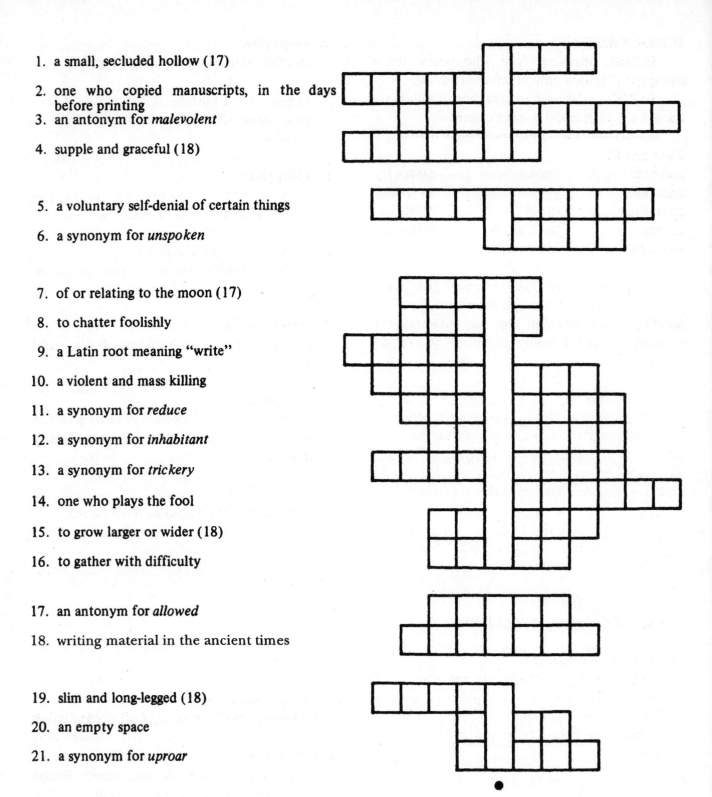

116

SCRIBE, meaning "one who writes for a newspaper," is used only in informal writing.

TABOO is also written *tabu*; both spellings are correct although *taboo* is more common.

Word List 20

ADJUNCT	EVINCE	SALINE
CHOLERIC	FEASIBLE	TANTALIZE
CONTAGIOUS	GLOSS	TRIBUNAL
ELLIPSE	METICULOUS	VEHEMENT
EMANATE	OTTOMAN	

Look up the words above in your dictionary. Note that some of the words have more than one meaning. When you feel that you know *all* the meanings of *all* the words, go on to the exercise below.

EXERCISE 20A

From the four choices under each phrase or sentence, you are to mark the one that is closest in meaning to the word appearing in italics. When the same word appears more than once, you should note that it is being used in a different sense.

1. to *emanate* from this spot
   (a) fall (b) issue forth (c) refuse to move (d) rise

2. a *saline* solution
   (a) acid (b) salt (c) strong (d) weak

3. to *tantalize* someone
   (a) ridicule by imitating the mannerisms of (b) play a trick on (c) torment by promising but withholding something from (d) make immune to disease by giving an injection to injection to

4. to draw an *ellipse*
   (a) rectangle (b) circle (c) square (d) oval

5. a *choleric* person
   (a) shortsighted (b) chronically sick (c) easiliy angered (d) sweet tempered

6. a high *gloss*
   (a) note (b) shine (c) mark (d) position

7. to *gloss* over a mistake
   (a) discover (b) make good (c) cover up (d) admit to

8. a long *gloss*
   (a) silk glove (b) set of instructions (c) explanatory note (d) animal skin

9. to *evince* a change of attitude
   (a) show (b) bring about (c) cover up (d) require

10. to *evince* a reply
    (a) require (b) call forth (c) listen for (d) make up

11. *contagious* diseases
    (a) restricted to the tropics (b) causing certain death (c) spreading rapidly (d) affecting children

12. a *meticulous* examination
    (a) thorough (b) brief (c) final (d) partial

13. a *vehement* accusation
    (a) joint (b) strong (c) false (d) fully documented

14. a *vehement* attack
    (a) surprise (b) ineffective (c) violent (d) armed

15. the *Ottoman* Empire
    (a) Roman (b) Turkish (c) British (d) Persian

16. a low *ottoman*
    (a) high-backed sofa (b) ornamental bridge (c) circular table (d) padded footstool

17. a member of the *tribunal*
    (a) bargaining committee (b) court of justice (c) three-person ruling council (d) group from which a jury is chosen

18. an *adjunct* to something
(a) informal invitation (b) farewell salute (c) non-essential addition (d) indirect approach

19. a *feasible* method
(a) impractical (b) old-fashioned (c) practical (d) modern

20. Her excuse doesn't seem *feasible*.
(a) fearsome (b) likely (c) necessary (d) expensive

Check your answers against the correct ones below. The answers are not in order; this is to prevent your eye from catching sight of the correct ones before you have had a chance to do the exercise on your own.

8c. 15b. 6b. 4d. 18c. 16d. 1b. 19c. 13b. 3c. 14c. 2b. 20b. 12a. 9a. 7c. 10b. 5c. 11c. 17b.

Go back to your dictionary and look up again those words for which you gave incorrect answers. Only after doing this should you go on to the next exercise.

EXERCISE 20B

Each word in Word List 20 is used four times in the following sentences; one of the sentences in each group uses the word incorrectly. You are to circle the letter that precedes that sentence. Do not circle more than one letter in any one group.

1. (a) Her plan sounds *feasible*, so I suggest we give it a try. (b) It's not *feasible* that he could have lied to us on this matter. (c) He's a *feasible* rogue, so don't let him talk you into giving him money. (d) We'll test the *feasibility* of her suggestion and report back to you.

2. (a) The drink she gave me tasted slightly of *vehement*. (b) The young man defended himself *vehemently* against the charges. (c) The president continued his policies despite the *vehement* opposition of Congress. (d) The *vehemence* of her argument took us all by surprise.

3. (a) The most *meticulous* attention to detail is required in this work. (b) The escape was *meticulously* planned and carried off with great boldness. (c) They assembled the model plane with great *meticulousness*. (d) The jacket was *meticulous* when I lent it to you, and now look at it; it's filthy!

4. (a) The outbreak of *choleric* in the area was quickly brought under control. (b) He was such a *choleric* old gentleman that no one wanted to argue with him. (c) She is no longer able to have things her own way, and this makes her *choleric*. (d) You must have angered him terribly for him to have such a *choleric* outburst.

5. (a) It was a *tantalizing* puzzle because it seemed so easy and yet so difficult. (b) He hinted about my birthday gift, but *tantalized* me by refusing to say more. (c) The thirsty desert explorers were *tantalized* by the thoughts of clear mountain streams. (d) The prisoners on the island were *tantalizingly* close to the mainland, but escape was impossible.

6. (a) The town was located at the *adjunct* of the two rivers. (b) Rhyme is no mere *adjunct* to poetry, but a vital part of it. (c) The vegetable garden was a useful *adjunct* to the farm. (d) An *adjunct* professor ranks below a full professor in most universities and colleges.

7. (a) He sat back in the armchair and put his feet up on the *ottoman*. (b) The *Ottoman* Empire collapsed shortly after the end of World War I. (c) The Greeks defeated the *Ottomans* in the war of 1821-1829. (d) Greek soldiers invaded *Ottoman* in their attempt to win freedom for their country.

8. (a) Persons having this disease should avoid contact with others because it is highly *contagious*. (b) The United States is *contagious* with Canada. (c) The laughter was *contagious*, and soon the whole room was in an uproar. (d) Chicken pox is a highly *contagious* disease.

118

9. (a) A lunar *ellipse* occurs when the moon is entirely in the earth's shadow. (b) A circle, viewed from a position not directly above it, appears to be an *ellipse*. (c) The *ellipse* had a diameter of 2 inches at its narrowest and 4 inches at its widest. (d) The planets move around the sun in slightly *elliptical* orbits.

10. (a) The *salinity* of seawater varies greatly from place to place. (b) The water has a slightly *saline* taste but is quite drinkable. (c) Gargling with a *saline* solution is a good remedy for a sore throat. (d) He was a *saline* old sea captain who had begun his career forty years ago.

11. (a) The Supreme Court is the highest *tribunal* in the land. (b) Members of the *tribunal* deliberated for two hours before reaching a verdict. (c) After serving as a county judge for twenty years, she was made a state *tribunal*. (d) The only *tribunal* she is answerable to is her own conscience.

12. (a) It will require strong evidence to *evince* me that she is guilty. (b) She *evinced* no pleasure at seeing me. (c) His talent for the piano *evinced* itself at an early age. (d) She could *evince* no satisfactory reply to the question.

13. (a) He tried to *gloss* over his mistake, but without success. (b) The cat's fur becomes *glossy* as the cold weather approaches. (c) The *gloss* at the bottom of the page explained the meaning of the term. (d) "I didn't do it," he *glossed* when we accused him of the theft.

14. (a) This order *emanated* from headquarters. (b) A delicate fragrance *emanated* from the flowers. (c) Her training and temperament make her *emanately* suitable for this position. (d) A good deal of the criticism of the mayor *emanates* from the candidates defeated in the election.

EXERCISE 20C

Rewrite each of the following sentences, replacing the italicized word or phrase with a word from Word List 20 and writing the word in the form that fits the rest of the sentence. Use each word only once. Write your answers in the spaces provided.

1. The smell seems to *come forth* from this *salt* solution.

....

....

2. The *low, cushioned footstool* is merely a *nonessential* addition to the armchair.

....

....

3. The members of the *court of justice* faced *intense and passionate* opposition to their verdict.

....

....

4. Doctors must be *attentive to every detail* in treating this disease since it is very *easily spread from person to person.*

....

....

5. She *showed* no interest in my plan although I am sure that it is quite *capable of being carried out.*

....

....

6. All day they *tormented him by offering him things but keeping them just out of reach from* him.

....

....

7. The *explanatory note* at the bottom of the page explained the formula for finding the area of a *perfectly symmetrical oval*.

....

....

8. He is a very *easily-angered* person, so be careful what you say to him.

....

....

EXERCISE 20D

In ancient and medieval times, it was believed that an individual's temperament was determined by the proportions in which various bodily fluids were present in his system. Our modern word CHOLERIC is derived from the belief that if a person had an excess of yellow bile, or *choler*, he became irritable and quick-tempered.

Define and explain the origin of each of the words below to show how these modern words are related to this ancient concept that the makeup of the human body and the "bodily fluids" are related to each person's temperament.

1. PHLEGMATIC

   definition ....

   ....

   ....

   origin ....

   ....

2. MELANCHOLY

   definition ....

   ....

....

origin ....

....

....

3. SANGUINE

   definition ....

   ....

   ....

   origin ....

   ....

   ....

4. GOOD-HUMORED

   definition ....

   ....

   ....

   origin ....

   ....

   ....

5. Explain the difference in meaning between *sanguine* and *sanguinary*.

   ....

   ....

   ....

   ....

EXERCISE 20E

Write out, in the spaces provided, the words from Word List 20 for which a definition, synonym, or antonym is given below. When you are asked to give a root or a prefix, you should refer back to the preceding exercise; the information you require will be found there. Make sure that each of your answers has the same number of letters as there are spaces. A definition followed by a number is a review word; the number gives the Word List from which it is taken.

If all the words are filled in correctly, the boxes running down the answer spaces will give the first five words of a quotation from the writings of Michel Eyquem de Montaigne, French essayist and man of letters, who was born in 1533 and died in 1592. The quotation will be continued in Exercise 21E.

1. boring and monotonous (15)

2. a ghostlike figure (16)

3. a secondary or nonessential addition

4. a perfectly symmetrical oval

5. a synonym for *possible*

6. a antonym for *careless*

7. showing great intensity of feeling

8. to cancel; to withdraw (17)

9. to torment by promising something but withholding it

10. spreading quickly from person to person

11. of, like, or containing salt

12. to show plainly

13. easily angered

14. to remove all moisture from (17)

15. explanatory note

16. of or relating to the Turks or Turkey

17. a place where one may remain undisturbed (18)

18. a court of law

19. stale and trite through overuse (14)

121

20. to be an example of (18)

21. to come forth; to issue

22. no longer having legal force (19)

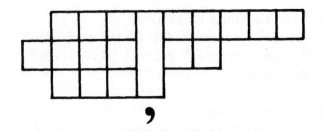

WORDLY WISE 20

Don't confuse CONTAGIOUS (pronounced *kon-TAY-jəs*), which means "spreading rapidly from person to person," with *contiguous* (pronounced *kon-TIG-yoo-əs*), which means "adjoining; touching."

An ELLIPSE is a perfectly symmetrical oval; don't confuse its plural form, *ellipses*, with *ellipsis* (Word List 15), "the intentional omission of a word or words."

Word List 21

ANTICLIMAX	IMPLICATION	PRETENTIOUS
CONSCIENTIOUS	INGENIOUS	PROFESS
COUNTERMAND	JIG	SYNTHESIS
EXTINGUISH	MISCREANT	TENUOUS
HYDRAULIC	POSTERITY	

Look up the words above in your dictionary. Note that some of the words have more than one meaning. When you feel that you know *all* the meanings of *all* the words, go on to the exercise below.

EXERCISE 21A

From the four choices under each phrase or sentence, you are to mark the one that is closest in meaning to the word appearing in italics. When the same word appears more than once, you should note that it is being used in a different sense.

1. a chemical *synthesis*
   (a) explosion (b) combining of elements (c) formula (d) chain reaction

2. to *profess* one's love
   (a) conceal (b) deny (c) declare (d) betray

3. to *countermand* an order
   (a) take steps to ensure compliance with (b) cancel by giving an opposite order (c) obtain approval for from one's chief (d) disobey by doing the exact opposite

4. a young *miscreant*
   (a) scholar (b) sportsman (c) hero (d) wrongdoer

5. a *tenuous* claim
   (a) legal (b) weak (c) moral (d) strong

6. *tenuous* air
   (a) not hazy (b) not pure (c) not clear (d) not dense

7. to understand the *implication*
   (a) reason for a course of action (b) thing suggested rather than stated (c) condition that is in effect (d) principle governing something

8. to *implicate* someone
   (a) insult (b) free (c) befriend (d) involve

9. a fast *jig*
   (a) two-wheeled carriage (b) lively dance (c) narrow racing boat (d) piece of sales talk

10. held in a *jig*
    (a) fit of terror that paralyzes one (b) device for guiding a tool (c) secluded area (d) device for restricting movement

11. a *conscientious* person
    (a) showing a heightened awareness (b) concerned to do what is right (c) in a trancelike state (d) lacking in concern for others

12. to *extinguish* the lights
    (a) set up (b) put out (c) barely be able to see (d) turn on

122

13. to do something for *posterity*
    (a) one's ancestors (b) future generations (c) considerations of personal gain (d) unselfish reasons

14. *pretentious* remarks
    (a) modest (b) self-important (c) deceitful (d) hostile

15. a *hydraulic* lift
    (a) operated by gravitational force (b) operated by muscle power (c) operated by fluid under pressure (d) operated by electric motors

16. *hydraulic* cement
    (a) hardening under water (b) hardening very quickly (c) reinforced with steel mesh (d) mixed with sand or gravel

17. to come as an *anticlimax*
    (a) welcome relief after much suffering (b) sudden transition from the significant to the trivial (c) answer to one's deepest prayers (d) logical consequence to what has gone before

18. an *ingenious* idea
    (a) clever (b) unworkable (c) vague (d) dangerous

Check your answers against the correct ones below. The answers are not in order; this is to prevent your eye from catching sight of the correct ones before you have had a chance to do the exercise on your own.

7b. 9b. 16a. 18a. 4d. 1b. 12b. 10b. 5b. 6d. 15c. 13b. 2c. 11b. 17b. 14b. 3b. 8d.

Go back to your dictionary and look up again those words for which you gave incorrect answers. Only after doing this should you go on to the next exercise.

EXERCISE 21B

Each word in Word List 21 is used four times in the following sentences; one of the sentences in each group uses the word incorrectly. You are to circle the letter that precedes that sentence. Do not circle more than one letter in any one group.

1. (a) The computer science students worked out an *ingenious* artificial intelligence program. (b) Leonardo da Vinci was an *ingenious* who excelled as a painter, sculptor, architect, and inventor. (c) It required great *ingenuity* to think up such a clever scheme. (d) Alexander Graham Bell was the *ingenious* inventor of the telephone.

2. (a) "Virginia Woolf and I share the same approach to writing," the young novelist said *pretentiously*. (b) It was a great shock to discover that the diamonds, which we had thought genuine, were actually *pretentious*. (c) A sixteen-room house with a swimming pool seems rather *pretentious*, so we will look for something smaller. (d) We were annoyed by her *pretentiousness* in offering to be our guide since she was a stranger to the district.

3. (a) We danced a *jig* around the room, we were so delighted at the news. (b) He picked up his old fiddle and played a lively *jig* for us. (c) They harnessed the horse to the *jig* and set off for the market. (d) The part is held firmly in the *jig*, and the drill is then brought onto it.

4. (a) The air above twenty thousand feet is so *tenuous* that oxygen masks must be worn. (b) The argument that we would have lost anyway is a *tenuous* one. (c) The spider spins its *tenuous* web in the most unlikely places. (d) She loved rock climbing, swimming, and other *tenuous* sports.

5. (a) It is polite to *profess* your hand to the person to whom you are introduced. (b) He *professed* a concern for our plight which he did not really feel. (c) The candidate is a *professed* conservative but hopes to get support from all sections of the party. (d) Despite his ardent *profession* of love for her, he never proposed marriage.

6. (a) I leave it to *posterity* to judge my worth as an artist. (b) The founders of the United States desired liberty for themselves and their *posterity*. (c) These forests must be preserved not only for ourselves but for *posterity*. (d) The lakes and forests are a part of our proud *posterity* that we must pass on to those who come after.

7. (a) She always made a *conscientious* effort to do the right thing. (b) She had suffered a severe blow to the head and was barely *conscientious* when we reached her. (c) The work was done *conscientiously*, in accordance with instructions. (d) A *conscientious* objector is a person whose conscience forbids him to go to war.

8. (a) I didn't fully realize the *implication* of her remarks. (b) He is suspected of *implication* in the robbery. (c) The *implication* I finally reached was that neither suspect was responsible. (d) Although you do not state it directly, the *implication* of your remarks is that I am lying.

9. (a) Water is the *synthesis* of hydrogen and oxygen. (b) Joy is the *synthesis* of sorrow, as love is of hate. (c) *Photosynthesis* is the forming of sugars and starches in plants from water and carbon dioxide due to the action of sunlight. (d) Opera is a *synthesis* of several different arts.

10. (a) "He loved Rembrandt, his country, and fudge sundaes," is an example of an *anticlimactic* statement. (b) After the brilliant successes of her youth, her obscurity in middle age came as an *anticlimax*. (c) The music builds to a thundering *anticlimax* that has the audience on the edge of their seats. (d) We waited breathlessly for the detective to name the murderer; instead, he *anticlimactically* announced that he was baffled.

11. (a) The brake cylinder needs a little more *hydraulic* added to it. (b) *Hydraulic* technology is based on the fact that fluids under pressure exert tremendous force. (c) *Hydraulic* cement, which hardens under water, is used in bridge supports and similar structures. (d) *Hydraulic* brakes are much safer than the mechanical brakes formerly used.

12. (a) The two colors are so similar that it is hard to *extinguish* between them. (b) Before leaving the campsite, make sure that your fire is *extinguished*. (c) Running out of money *extinguished* my hope of going to Europe. (d) All opposition to his rule was *extinguished* by the jailing of all who did not affirm their loyalty.

13. (a) The *miscreants* were led before the judge for sentencing. (b) He preferred being a *miscreant* to working at an honest job. (c) Criminals should be rehabilitated so that they will no longer *miscreant* innocent people. (d) Treating these young *miscreants* as criminals is too harsh; they broke your window accidentally.

14. (a) The two leaders did not get along and were constantly *countermanding* each other's orders. (b) This preparation rapidly *countermands* the effects of the poison. (c) This order *countermands* all earlier instructions on this subject. (d) The company president *countermanded* my boss's orders, leaving me totally confused.

EXERCISE 21C

Rewrite each of the following sentences, replacing the italicized word or phrase with a word from Word List 21 and writing the word in the form that fits the rest of the sentence. Use each word only once. Write your answers in the spaces provided.

1. The plot of this novel is *flimsy and unsubstantial*, and its ending comes as an *abrupt transition from the significant to the trivial*.

. . . .

. . . .

2. She claims, somewhat *pompously and self-importantly*, that her books will be read by *future generations*.

. . . .

. . . .

3. Make sure that the *device used to guide the tool* is fastened firmly before you begin drilling.

. . . .

. . . .

4. A camper who is truly *concerned about doing what is right* takes care to *put out* her campfire before leaving.

. . . .

. . . .

5. This *wrongdoer* has the gall to *openly declare* her innocence when we all know that she is guilty.

. . . .

. . . .

6. The new elevators being installed will be *operated by fluids under pressure.*

. . . .

. . . .

7. The *suggestion, indirectly stated,* was that I had *given orders that were contrary to* her instructions.

. . . .

. . . .

8. The *combining into a whole* of the various elements was accomplished in an *original and clever* manner.

. . . .

EXERCISE 21D

The Greek prefix *anti-* means "against" or "opposite" (an ANTICLIMAX is the opposite of a *climax*). A similar sounding prefix is the Latin *ante-,* which means "before" or "in front of."

Complete the words or phrases below by adding either the Greek prefix *anti-* or the Latin prefix *ante-.* Write a brief definition of each.

1. _____BELLUM . . . .

. . . .

. . . .

2. _____ROOM . . . .

. . . .

. . . .

3. _____THESIS . . . .

. . . .

. . . .

4. _____CEDENT . . . .

. . . .

. . . .

5. _____SEPTIC . . . .

. . . .

. . . .

6. _____PODES . . . .

. . . .

. . . .

7. _____ ARCTIC . . . .

. . . .

. . . .

8. _____ DATE . . . .

. . . .

. . . .

9. _____ DOTE . . . .

. . . .

. . . .

10. _____ MERIDIEM . . . .

. . . .

. . . .

EXERCISE 21E

Write out, in the spaces provided, the words from Word List 21 for which a definition, synonym, or antonym is given. When you are asked to give a root or a prefix, you should refer back to the preceding exercise; the information you require will be found there. Make sure that each of your answers has the same number of letters as there are spaces. A definition followed by a number is a review word; the number gives the Word List from which it is taken.

If all the words are filled in correctly, the boxes running down the answer spaces will continue the quotation begun earlier.

1. a person who acts the fool (19)

2. a synonym for *clever*

3. a synonym for *wrongdoer*

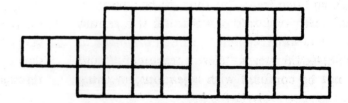

4. to cancel a command by giving one that is opposite

5. lasting but a day (11)

6. to declare openly

7. an antonym for *dense*

8. a fast, lively dance

9. to avoid (10)

10. the combining of parts into a whole

11. done with concern to what is right

12. an abrupt transition from the significant to the trivial

13. widespread (15)

14. an antonym for *light* (verb)

15. an antonym for *humble*

16. a feeling of well-being (14)

17. a Greek prefix meaning "against"

18. to come or bring together (11)

19. operated by fluid under pressure

20. something that strengthens or protects (9)

21. future generations

22. something suggested rather than openly stated

WORDLY WISE 21

IMPLICATION is the noun form of two verbs: *imply*, "to indicate without saying openly" (I resent the *implication* in your remarks that I did nothing), and *implicate*, "to show to be a party to a crime." (His *implication* in the plot was proved beyond any doubt.)

INGENIOUS means "clever; resourceful" and should not be confused with *ingenuous*, meaning "simple and open; naively frank."

Don't confuse JIG and *gig* (Word List 3). A *jig* is (1) a fast, lively dance, or the music for such a dance, and (2) a device for guiding a machine tool. A *gig* is (1) a light ship's boat, (2) a two-wheeled, horse-drawn carriage, and (3) a job. Both words are verbs as well: to *jig* is to perform such a fast, lively dance and to *gig* is to catch fish by trailing hooks through the water.

Across

1. a violent and bloody mass killing
4. a secondary or nonessential addition
11. operating by fluid under pressure
12. strictly forbidden
13. to collect or gather bit by bit
15. concerned to do what is right
17. lacking density; rarified; thin
19. showing cleverness or originality
22. of or relating to the Turks or Turkey
24. a perfectly symmetrical oval
25. easily angered
28. to reduce the importance of
29. to help, especially in wrongdoing (4)
30. capable of being done; possible
31. inclined to do good; kindly
33. lacking sophistication; crude (2)
35. to chatter foolishly
38. trickery; deception
39. making exaggerated claims; self-important
42. a person who acts the fool
43. to do away with; to cancel (17)
44. future generations
45. the combining of parts into a whole
46. to put out; to put an end to

Down

1. with great attention to detail; thorough
2. of, like, or containing salt
3. an abrupt transition from the significant to the trivial
5. a fast, lively dance
6. to punish, especially by beating (2)
7. a court of justice
8. an explanatory note
9. one who copied manuscripts in medieval times
10. spreading quickly from person to person
14. to cancel a command by giving another
16. to show plainly
18. a villain; a wrongdoer
20. an inhabitant
21. moving from one region to another (17)
23. to torment by holding back what is promised
26. something suggested rather than stated
27. a voluntary self-denial of certain things
32. showing intensity of feeling; passionate
33. a writing material of the ancient world
34. an empty space
35. to declare openly
36. to come forth; to issue
37. enraged behavior; an uproar
40. implied but not stated; unspoken
41. a fixed, mechanical way of learning (1)

128

Chapter Eight

Word List 22

ACCUMULATE	DEITY	PORTAGE
BALK	EXACT	SECEDE
BEGUILE	IMMOBILE	SENILE
COMPASSION	LINEAMENT	SUSTENANCE
CONTRAVENE	PLAGIARISM	TURGID

Look up the words above in your dictionary. Note that some of the words have more than one meaning. When you feel that you know *all* the meanings of *all* the words, go on to the exercise below.

EXERCISE 22A

From the four choices under each phrase or sentence, you are to mark the one that is closest in meaning to the word appearing in italics. When the same word appears more than once, you should note that it is being used in a different sense.

1. to *balk*
   (a) lend support and encouragement (b) abruptly refuse to act (c) act in an offensive manner (d) pretend to launch an attack

2. *balked* by someone
   (a) encouraged (b) stopped (c) insulted (d) cheated

3. *turgid* language
   (a) simple (b) technical (c) poetic (d) pompous

4. *turgid* limbs
   (a) muscular (b) stiff (c) swollen (d) twisted

5. to be *senile*
   (a) in a position of authority (b) weak after an illness (c) unduly humble before others (d) weak from old age

6. to feel *compassion*
   (a) joy (b) sympathy (c) anger (d) envy

7. the *lineaments* of his face
   (a) exaggerated drawings (b) candid photographs (c) distinctive features (d) changing expressions

8. to remain *immobile*
   (a) unconvinced (b) motionless (c) dissatisfied (d) unprotected

9. to *secede*
   (a) withdraw from an organization (b) follow next in line (c) agree to another's demands (d) surrender a legal claim

10. to *contravene* the law
    (a) cancel (b) abide by (c) bring up to date (d) go against

11. to *beguile* someone
    (a) threaten (b) deceive (c) reward (d) discourage

12. a *beguiling* companion
    (a) knowledgeable (b) charming (c) mysterious (d) offensive

13. to *accumulate* wealth
    (a) spend foolishly (b) scorn (c) pile up (d) worship

14. *exact* measurements
    (a) approximate (b) precise (c) incorrect (d) unknown

15. to *exact* obedience
    (a) expect (b) demand (c) scorn (d) have a high regard for

16. an *exacting* employer
    (a) lax (b) strict (c) unfair (d) generous

17. a long *portage*

(a) artificial dock for small boats (b) overland route between navigable waterways (c) dried-up riverbed used as a trail (d) procession of small boats before a race

18. to provide *sustenance*

(a) police protection (b) legal proof (c) nourishment (d) financial support

19. accused of *plagiarism*

(a) holding ideas contrary to those held officially (b) passing off another's work as one's own (c) stealing money entrusted to one's care (d) attaching too much importance to social position

20. a Greek *deity*

(a) temple (b) god (c) law (d) court

Check your answers against the correct ones below. The answers are not in order; this is to prevent your eye from catching sight of the correct ones before you have had a chance to do the exercise on your own.

7c. 9a. 16b. 18c. 4c. 1b. 12b. 10d. 5d. 19b. 20b. 6b. 15b. 13c. 2b. 11b. 17b. 14b. 3d. 8b.

Go back to your dictionary and look up again those words for which you gave incorrect answers. Only after doing this should you go on to the next exercise.

EXERCISE 22B

Each word in Word List 22 is used four times in the following sentences; one of the sentences in each group uses the word incorrectly. You are to circle the letter that precedes that sentence. Do not circle more than one letter in any one group.

1. (a) This essay on **Macbeth** has been *plagiarized* from the introduction to the play. (b) If she stole your ideas and passed them off as her own, she is guilty of *plagiarism*. (c) Bubonic plague *plagiarized* Europe for centuries before it was wiped out. (d) The man is an impudent *plagiarist* who simply rewrote my book under his own name.

2. (a) She has *accumulated* a fine collection of rare first editions. (b) The professor *accumulated* the papers from the students and began grading them. (c) Every few weeks we clean out the junk that has *accumulated* in the basement. (d) By the end of the week, there was an *accumulation* of five feet of snow on the slopes.

3. (a) On the death of the earl, his eldest son *seceded* to the title. (b) Those members who disagreed with the policies of the church were free to *secede* from it. (c) The *secession* of the southern states from the Federal Union led to the War between the States. (d) The *secessionists* who argued that the South should withdraw from the Union finally had their way.

4. (a) The man had become *senile* and now found familiar things confusing. (b) She was in her late eighties, yet showed no signs of *senility*. (c) The party is controlled by people who have grown *senile* in office, and new blood is urgently needed. (d) Those members who are beginning to *senile* should be replaced by younger people.

5. (a) Since people draw their *sustenance* from the soil, they must guard against exhausting it. (b) Just fifty cents a day provides *sustenance* for a starving child in Asia. (c) Their sole *sustenance* during their ordeal was a chocolate bar and a canteen of water. (d) Good discipline in a classroom is necessary for the *sustenance* of the lesson.

6. (a) She was a simple person, utterly lacking in *beguile*. (b) They were *beguiled* into surrendering by promises of fair treatment. (c) They *beguiled* the night away with talk of the good old days. (d) So *beguiling* were our companions that the evening passed in a flash.

7. (a) No law should be passed which *contravenes* those already on the statute book. (b) I have no desire to *contravene* in what is obviously a private dispute. (c) You deliberately acted in

contravention to the instructions you were given. (d) Anyone *contravening* these instructions will be answerable to me personally.

8. (a) Have *compassion* for those less fortunate than yourself. (b) Nurses must be efficient and *compassionate* at the same time. (c) The novel deals with the *compassionate* love affair between Lord Nelson and Lady Hamilton. (d) The soldier was granted a week's leave on *compassionate* grounds when his mother died.

9. (a) We should get down on our knees and thank the *Deity* for His help. (b) This book questions the *deity* of Christ and claims that he was merely a great teacher. (c) The Hindu religion, with its thousands of different *deities*, can be confusing to non-Hindus. (d) The Romans' attempts to *deity* their emperor were unsuccessful.

10. (a) The *exact* sciences, such as astronomy and physics, are those with laws capable of precise quantitative expression. (b) She *exacted* a very high price for her support. (c) Due to the *exacting* demands of this work, persons are allowed a thirty-minute break every two hours. (d) She *exacted* violently when I broke the news to her.

11. (a) Our planes have been *immobilized* for two nights because of the bad weather. (b) The entire labor union *immobilized* to help support our requests for change. (c) Her features remained *immobile* despite the great mental strain she was undergoing. (d) The deer stood *immobile*, hypnotized by the glare of the headlights.

12. (a) The governor *balked* at signing such a poorly organized bill. (b) The project was *balked* by the failure of the public to lend its support. (c) I was willing to try the frogs' legs but *balked* at eating snails. (d) The woman's family recieved small sums, but the *balk* of the estate went to charity.

13. (a) Between the two rivers was a *portage* of some ten miles in length. (b) Their supplies included some two hundred pounds of *portage*. (c) A small fort had been established to guard the *portage* between the Fox and Wisconsin rivers. (d) The water route to the Columbia River was 1200 miles long with some twenty *portages*.

14. (a) The portrait artist had captured with extraordinary skill the bold *lineaments* of his face. (b) He rubbed *lineament* into his bruised and aching muscles. (c) The aged *lineaments* of the old man's face were set in an attitude of repose. (d) Still beautiful at fifty, she falsely believed she needed makeup to smooth the *lineaments* of her face.

15. (a) In a *turgid* speech that went on far too long, she praised the efforts of the president. (b) Her face was red and slightly *turgid* from her bad sunburn. (c) He moved in such a *turgid* manner that I thought he was ill. (d) The contrast in the book between the racy dialogue and the *turgid* narrative passages is particularly marked.

EXERCISE 22C

Rewrite each of the following sentences, replacing the italicized word or phrase with a word from Word List 22 and writing the word in the form that fits the rest of the sentence. Use each word only once. Write your answers in the spaces provided.

1. Their plan to *withdraw themselves* from the organization was *held up* by a lack of sufficient funds.

. . . .

. . . .

2. He is so *weak from old age* that he arouses only *feelings of sympathy and pity* in me.

. . . .

. . . .

3. The Japanese emperor was worshipped as a *godlike figure* by the people.

   . . . .

   . . . .

4. She remained *perfectly still*, the *distinctive features* of her face seeming to be carved out of stone.

   . . . .

   . . . .

5. The only passages not written in his usual *pompous and puffed up* style are those he has *stolen from other writers and passed off as his own*.

   . . . .

   . . . .

6. By *gradually building up* such a large supply of gold, you have *acted contrary to* the law.

   . . . .

   . . . .

7. He *demanded and got* a heavy price for the *nourishing and strength-giving foods* he supplied to us.

   . . . .

   . . . .

8. They were *deceived* into believing that the *overland route between the two navigable waterways* was much shorter than it actually was.

   . . . .

   . . . .

   . . . .

EXERCISE 22D

The roots italicized in the words below are derived from Greek and Latin numbers. Look up each word in a dictionary that gives word origins and write the meaning of each root. State whether the root is Latin (L) or Greek (Gr) in origin.

	meaning	origin
1. *quint*et	. . . .	. . . . .
2. *bi*weekly	. . . .	. . . . .
3. *deci*mate	. . . .	. . . . .
4. *uni*verse	. . . .	. . . . .
5. *hemi*sphere	. . . .	. . . . .
6. *tetra*meter	. . . .	. . . . .
7. *milli*gram	. . . .	. . . .
8. *nov*ena	. . . .	. . . .
9. *tri*plets	. . . .	. . . .
10. *oct*ave	. . . .	. . . .
11. *mono*logue	. . . .	. . . . .
12. *cent*ury	. . . .	. . . . .
13. *sex*tet	. . . .	. . . . .
14. *du*plicate	. . . .	. . . . .
15. *deca*de	. . . .	. . . . .
16. *quad*rangle	. . . .	. . . . . .
17. *demi*god	. . . .	. . . . . .
18. *mono*cle	. . . .	. . . . .
19. *hecto*meter	. . . .	. . . . .
20. *hexa*gon	. . . .	. . . . .

21. *kilo*gram ....

22. *uni*form ....

23. *Octo*ber ....

24. *penta*gram ....

EXERCISE 22E

Write out, in the spaces provided, the words from Word List 22 for which a definition, synonym, or antonym is given below. When you are asked to give a root or a prefix, you should refer back to the preceding exercise; the information you require will be found there. Make sure that each of your answers has the same number of letters as there are spaces. A definition followed by a number is a review word; the number gives the Word List from which it is taken.

If all the words are filled in correctly, the boxes running down the answer spaces will conclude the quotation begun in Exercise 20E.

1. with a humorous twist (18)

2. a carrying of boats and supplies between navigable water

3. to act contrary to

4. a distinctive feature, as of the face

5. quick-tempered; easily-angered (20)

6. that which nourishes or gives strength

7. an antonym for *dissipate*

8. the passing off of another's work as one's own

9. to abruptly refuse to act

10. to demand and get

11. a synonym for *pity*

12. to deceive into doing something

13. to declare openly (21)

14. a synonym for *swollen*

15. of, like or containing salt (20)

16. a synonym for *still*

17. a god or godlike figure

133

18. cheap-looking and showy (16)

19. strictly forbidden (19)

20. a particular region or area (1)

21. concerned to do what is right (21)

22. feeble from old age

23. to withdraw, as from an organization

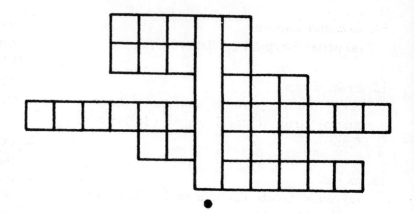

WORDLY WISE 22

Don't confuse LINEAMENT, "a distinctive feature, as of the face," with *liniment*, "an ointment rubbed into the skin to ease soreness."

Word List 23

BADGER	FORMAT	PLIGHT
DURESS	IMMACULATE	PROTÉGÉ
ENCOMPASS	IOTA	PSEUDONYM
EXUDE	MAGNANIMOUS	SEDATE
FLACCID	PEDANTIC	TENACIOUS

Look up the words above in your dictionary. Note that some of the words have more than one meaning. When you feel that you know *all* the meanings of *all* the words, go on to the exercise below.

EXERCISE 23A

From the four choices under each phrase or sentence, you are to mark the one that is closest in meaning to the word appearing in italics. When the same word appears more than once, you should note that it is being used in a different sense.

1. to be *tenacious*
   (a) given to arguing (b) gripping firmly (c) following a winding path (d) lacking in density

2. *immaculate* linen
   (a) bed (b) spotless (c) soiled (d) table

3. a *pedantic* person
   (a) gracefully witty (b) wise (c) who stresses trivial points of learning (d) curious

4. to be *magnanimous*

(a) agreed to by all (b) outrageously rude (c) pompously exaggerated (d) bighearted

5. to *encompass* both views
   (a) disagree with (b) include (c) listen to (d) exclude

6. to *encompass* the enemy
   (a) defeat (b) pursue (c) surround (d) engage

7. under a *pseudonym*
   (a) guarantee of safety (b) veil of secrecy (c) cloud of suspicion (d) false name

8. in a *plight*
   (a) pleasant frame of mind (b) position of trust (c) angry mood (d) difficult situation

9. a young *protégé*
   (a) person convicted of a criminal offense (b) person guided and helped by another (c) person who rebels against authority (d) person who shows extraordinary ability

10. *flaccid* muscles
    (a) firm (b) flabby (c) stretched (d) knotted

11. a *sedate* manner
    (a) suspicious (b) violent (c) calm (d) humorous

12. to *exude* moisture
    (a) soak up (b) give off (c) collect (d) dry up

13. a young *badger*
    (a) social climber (b) broad-backed burrowing animal (c) ruffian (d) web-footed amphibian

14. to *badger* someone
(a) pester (b) ignore (c) flatter (d) insult

15. under *duress*
(a) the most favorable conditions (b) great mental strain (c) medical care (d) threat of force

16. an *iota*
(a) gentle breeze (b) note of thanks (c) tiny amount (d) slight pause

17. the *format* of something
(a) beginning (b) makeup (c) development (d) end

Check your answers against the correct ones below. The answers are not in order; this is to prevent your eye from catching sight of the correct ones before you have had a chance to do the exercise on your own.

15d. 4d. 8d. 7d. 17b. 12b. 6c. 1b. 10b. 11c. 2b. 5b. 13b. 14a. 16c. 3c. 9b.

Go back to your dictionary and look up again those words for which you gave incorrect answers. Only after doing this should you go on to the next exercise.

EXERCISE 23B
Each word in Word List 23 is used four times in the following sentences; one of the sentences in each group uses the word incorrectly. You are to circle the letter that precedes that sentence. Do not circle more than one letter in any one group.

1. (a) The air is so *tenacious* at these altitudes that oxygen masks must be worn. (b) One cannot help admiring the stubborn *tenacity* with which they cling to their beliefs. (c) The shipwrecked sailors clung *tenaciously* to the raft. (d) He has a *tenacious* memory and can recall in detail events that occurred years ago.

2. (a) There was nothing for the censors to criticize in the *immaculate* lives of the characters in the book. (b) The people who had rented the house from us left it in *immaculate* condition. (c) She *immaculated* from college at the age of nineteen. (d) We were horrified when the waiter spilled soup down his *immaculate* shirt front.

3. (a) He is a *pedant*, forever correcting the slightest errors of his colleagues. (b) I ignored the *pedantics* of my opponent and continued with my speech. (c) She is the world's leading authority in her field, yet she is not in the least *pedantic*. (d) The author's fine concern for scholarship occasionally lapses into *pedantry*.

4. (a) He was too *magnanimous* to resent the wrongs that had been done him. (b) She bore her troubles with a *magnanimity* that impressed us all. (c) The resolution would have passed *magnanimously* but for one dissenting vote. (d) She *magnanimously* refused to press charges against the newspaper that had slandered her.

5. (a) The course *encompasses* all the various branches of modern philosophy. (b) The *encompassment* of the enemy position was achieved under cover of darkness. (c) The navigator *encompassed* our position as fifty miles east of Bermuda. (d) The Mojave Desert is *encompassed* by mountain ranges.

6. (a) He donned dark glasses and a false moustache as a *pseudonym*. (b) The book was written *pseudonymously*, and its author is still unknown. (c) "Mark Twain" was the *pseudonym* employed by Samuel L. Clemens. (d) She wrote several *pseudonymous* works in addition to many books under her own name.

7. (a) The *plight* of these starving people is receiving considerable attention in the press. (b) She had accidentally locked herself in the closet, and her *plight* was not discovered for some time. (c) Our hopes were *plighted* by their refusal to come to our aid. (d) In the parlor of the little cottage they *plighted* their troth.

8. (a) He was a struggling beginner in the golf world when he became the *protégé* of the world champion. (b) The long *protégé* of mourners filed past the coffin. (c) The senator has promised to support his *protégé* in the coming election. (d) He had been a *protégé* of the famed conductor Arturo Toscanini and went on to win considerable acclaim as a musician.

9. (a) *Flaccid* is spun into linen thread on these machines. (b) The book's *flaccid* prose deters even the most eager reader. (c) His muscles had grown *flaccid* during his long illness. (d) The *flaccidity* of their leadership contributed in large measure to their defeat.

10. (a) Grandmother was a *sedate* old lady who protested when we drove over 40 miles per hour. (b) The *sedate* atmosphere of the hotel makes it more suited to those who prefer quiet. (c) The doctor gave him a mild *sedate* to calm his nerves. (d) She sat down *sedately*, heedless of the uproar her entrance had created.

11. (a) He *exuded* confidence before the start of the race. (b) The pot of stew *exuded* a delicious aroma. (c) A sticky substance *exuded* from the tree where the branch had been pulled off. (d) "I've won!" she *exuded* joyfully when the results were announced.

12. (a) The reporters *badgered* her with questions until she almost lost her temper. (b) That was a cruel *badger* they played on that little boy. (c) *Badgers* are able to tunnel underground with great speed. (d) I can't go anywhere these days without someone *badgering* me for money.

13. (a) The hero, under *duress*, confesses to the crime of which he is innocent. (b) A population under the *duress* of a dictatorship will be less productive than a free people. (c) Since this confession was obtained under *duress*, it cannot be admitted as evidence. (d) The defendant claims she was *duressed* into taking part in the robbery.

14. (a) During a slight *iota* in the conversation, I managed to ask my question. (b) He doesn't have an *iota* of common sense. (c) There is not an *iota* of truth in what she says. (d) He had not an *iota* of statesmanship.

15. (a) The *format* of the magazine may be changed to allow for more pictures. (b) The airmail stamps are of triangular *format* and are much prized by collectors. (c) The planes flew over the base in a V-shaped *format*. (d) The *format* of the show strikes a balance between comedy and musical numbers.

EXERCISE 23C

Rewrite each of the sentences below, replacing the italicized word or phrase with a word from Word List 23 and writing the word in the form that fits the rest of the sentence. Use each word only once. Write your answers in the spaces provided.

1. The *young artist who had received the help and support* of the great musician walked *in a calm and dignified manner* onto the stage and began to play.

   . . . .

   . . . .

2. The leadership of the company is *soft and flabby* and *gives off* an air of failure.

   . . . .

   . . . .

3. Under an *assumed name* he wrote several books on the *difficult situation* of the Native Americans.

   . . . .

   . . . .

4. I found her to be a *generous and lofty-spirited* person, with a soul as *pure and spotless* as a saint's.

....
....

5. She clung *firmly and persistently* to her story even though she knew there was not one *tiny bit* of truth in it.

....
....

6. We *kept on pestering* him until he agreed to change the *general arrangement* of the magazine.

....
....

7. Her reading *includes* a wide range of topics.

....
....

8. I agreed, but only under *threat of force*, that the professor is *fond of emphasizing trivial points of learning*.

....
....

EXERCISE 23D

The ninth letter in the Greek alphabet is written *ι* and is called *iota*. Since it is the smallest letter in the Greek alphabet, a tiny or almost non-existent amount has come to be called an IOTA ("There is not an *iota* of truth in what he says" means that there is no truth in what he says).

Explain the origin of each of the following terms in similar manner to that above. Use a dictionary or, preferably, a reference book of word origins to find your answers.

1. TANTALIZE

....

....
....
....

2. PAPER

....
....
....
....

3. TITANIC

....
....
....
....

4. DELTA

....
....
....
....

EXERCISE 23E

Write out, in the spaces provided, the words from Word List 23 for which a definition, synonym, or antonym is given on the next page. When you are asked to give a root or a prefix, you should refer to the preceding exercise; the information you need will be found there. Make sure that each of your answers has the same number of letters as there are spaces. A definition followed by a number is a review word; the number gives the Word List from which it is taken.

If all the words are filled in correctly, the boxes running down the answer spaces will give the first six words of a short quotation taken from the Book of Proverbs in the Old Testament.

1. threat of force; compulsion

2. to act contrary to (22)

3. a synonym for *pester*

4. an antonym for *small-minded*

5. a synonym for *persistent*

6. a general makeup or arrangement

7. one who receives the support and guidance of another

8. a tiny amount

9. a synonym for *flabby*

10. an alloy of tin and lead (18)

11. light and airy; delicate (18)

12. an antonym for *frantic*

13. emphasizing trivial points of learning

14. a difficult or dangerous situation

15. to give off

16. brief and full of meaning (14)

17. a synonym for *enclose*

18. a synonym for *spotless*

19. a fictitious or assumed name

20. feeble from old age (22)

FLACCID is pronounced *FLAK-sid*; an alternative but less common pronunciation is *FLAS-id*.

PLIGHT, in addition to meaning "a difficult or dangerous situation," is also a verb meaning "to promise; to pledge." It survives in this meaning only in the phrase "to plight one's troth," meaning "to become engaged to be married." Note that this expression is archaic and rarely used.

PROTÉGÉ (pronounced *PRO-tə-zhay*) is a French word and must be spelled with an acute accent over each "e."

Word List 24

AMBLE	INCARCERATE	SATIETY
AMPUTATE	INCISION	SPASM
DREGS	NOXIOUS	SPECIFIC
EXTRICATE	PENDULOUS	TOTALITARIAN
ILLICIT	PROVISIONAL	TRAIT

Look up the words above in your dictionary. Note that some of the words have more than one meaning. When you feel that you know *all* the meanings of *all* the words, go on to the exercise below.

EXERCISE 24A

From the four choices under each phrase or sentence, you are to mark the one that is closest in meaning to the word appearing in italics. When the same word appears more than once, you should note that it is being used in a different sense.

1. to *extricate* a person
   (a) hand over to another state (b) destroy completely (c) release from some difficulty (d) demand money by threats from

2. a *provisional* government
   (a) duly elected (b) benevolent (c) temporary (d) local

3. a violent *spasm*
   (a) fight with many people participating (b) involuntary tightening of a muscle (c) scene in a play, book, or movie (d) speech attacking a person or thing

4. a *spasm* of fear
   (a) sudden cry (b) glazed look (c) total lack (d) sudden, brief feeling

5. a feeling of *satiety*
   (a) gnawing hunger (b) bitter disappointment (c) having had too much (d) having done something wrong

6. an *illicit* act
   (a) unhurried (b) unkind (c) unlawful (d) unnoticed

7. to be *specific*
   (a) definite (b) spiteful (c) uncertain (d) generous

8. a suggested *specific*
   (a) outline (b) plan of attack (c) method (d) remedy

9. an admirable *trait*
   (a) original idea (b) detailed explanation (c) distinguishing characteristic (d) act of unselfishness

10. *pendulous* branches
    (a) thickly-leaved (b) dried-out (c) thick (d) drooping

11. a long *incision*
    (a) mark left after a wound has healed (b) piece of inserted material (c) front tooth used for biting (d) cut, often made by a surgeon

12. to *amble* back
    (a) hurry (b) stroll (c) grow (d) fall

13. to *amputate* a leg
    (a) bandage tightly (b) remove surgically (c) apply splints to (d) injure severely

14. *noxious* fumes
    (a) heavy (b) harmful (c) colorless (d) odorless

15. the *dregs* of society
    (a) upper classes (b) least valuable (c) commonly accepted rules (d) fashionable leaders

16. *dregs* of wine
    (a) small glasses (b) small barrels (c) sediment (d) flavor

17. a *totalitarian* country
    (a) conquered and governed by a foreign invader (b) enclosed on all its borders by other countries (c) governed by a single leader or political party having complete control (d) in which the citizens do exactly as they please

18. to *incarcerate* someone
    (a) trick (b) imprison (c) pretend to be (d) release

Check your answers against the correct ones below. The answers are not in order; this is to prevent your eye from catching sight of the correct ones before you have had a chance to do the exercise on your own.

3b. 9c. 5c. 13b. 14b. 16c. 1c. 10d. 11d. 2c. 7a. 17c. 12b. 18b. 6c. 15b. 4d. 8d.

Go back to your dictionary and look up again those words for which you gave incorrect answers. Only after doing this should you go on to the next exercise.

EXERCISE 24B

Each word in Word List 24 is used four times in the following sentences; one of the sentences in each group uses the word incorrectly. You are to circle the letter that precedes that sentence. Do not circle more than one letter in any one group.

1. (a) If found guilty, he could be *incarcerated* in the state prison for five years. (b) All garbage, except for cans and bottles, is thrown into the *incarcerator* and burned. (c) She found it hard to get a job following her *incarceration* for ten years in the penitentiary. (d) At the infamous Black Hole of Calcutta, 143 men were *incarcerated* in a room 18 feet by 14 feet.

2. (a) They lived in an *amble* little cottage at the end of the lane. (b) On Sundays when the weather is fine, we go for an *amble* in the

woods. (c) We *ambled* down the lane, listening to the song of the birds. (d) The horses *ambled* up to the starting gate and got into position for the big race.

3. (a) The *pendulous* jowls of the old bloodhound shook when he barked. (b) The *pendulous* branches of the willow tree trailed gracefully in the water. (c) The heavy rope tied to the beam swung *pendulously* in the breeze. (d) She wrote the letter with a *pendulous* heart and signed it with a sigh.

4. (a) We were gorged to *satiety* after the huge meal and wanted only to sleep. (b) He was able to reduce his *satiety* by eating smaller meals. (c) The book aroused the reader's interest and satisfies it but does not *satiate* it. (d) The guests, thoroughly *satiated*, at last rose from the table and retired to their rooms.

5. (a) With some difficulty he managed to *extricate* the package from the crevice into which it had fallen. (b) The carriage was stuck in the mud, and there was no one at hand to *extricate* it. (c) Weaving the subtle pattern variations into the rug was an extremely *extricate* task. (d) She managed to *extricate* herself from what could have been an embarrassing situation.

6. (a) People living under a *totalitarian* form of government have no power to recall their leader. (b) You cannot *totalitarian* these people into obeying those whom they despise. (c) The *totalitarian* rule of Joseph Stalin brought suffering to millions of Russians. (d) *Totalitarian* governments took power in Germany, Italy, and Spain during the 1920s and '30s.

7. (a) Her *noxious* behavior at the party offended the guests. (b) The entire world was repelled by the *noxious* philosophy of the Nazi rulers. (c) *Noxious* wastes discharged into the river are killing the fish. (d) Car engines had filled the garage with *noxious* exhaust fumes.

140

8. (a) We cannot tolerate *incision* on your part; you must make up your mind. (b) The surgeon made a six-inch *incision* just below the patient's rib cage. (c) With a stroke of her scalpel, the doctor *incised* the swollen tissue. (d) Thirty stitches were needed to close the *incision* in the patient's abdomen.

9. (a) Aspirin is a widely used *specific* for headaches. (b) With his powerful telescope he was able to *specify* a small ship on the horizon. (c) You promise to see me some time in the future, but can you be more *specific* than that? (d) The drug has certain *specific* qualities that make it suitable for treating this disease.

10. (a) *Spasms* of pain shot through her body whenever she tried to move. (b) His chest heaved in a violent *spasm* as he tried to draw breath. (c) The boat *spasmed* sharply to the left to avoid the rocks. (d) She twitched *spasmodically* for a few moments, then lay still.

11. (a) The *dregs* from the guests' cups were emptied into the sink. (b) He lived among the *dregs* of society for a while to get material for a book. (c) The oil is poured carefully so as to leave the *dregs* at the bottom. (d) The wine was stored in small *dregs*.

12. (a) The survivor on the desert island was *amputated* from all human contact for over two years. (b) The *amputation* of the diseased limb took less than a minute. (c) In this hospital *amputees* are taught the use of artificial limbs. (d) Her leg had turned gangrenous, and the only hope was for the doctors to *amputate*.

13. (a) If he was willing to *trait* his country, then he deserves to be punished. (b) A sense of humor is her strongest *trait*. (c) He possessed that rare *trait*, the ability to laugh at himself. (d) A selfish lack of concern for others is one of her less admirable *traits*.

14. (a) The *illicit* use of dangerous drugs continues despite severe penalties. (b) I was unable to *illicit* any response to my questions. (c) The men were charged with making whiskey in an *illicit* still that they kept on the farm. (d) The money raised for campaign funds was transferred *illicitly* to her private account.

15. (a) The *provisional* government will hold power until free elections can be held. (b) This assessment of the situation is *provisional* and subject to change when fresh facts are available. (c) The captain was attached *provisionally* to headquarters while awaiting assignment elsewhere. (d) They had brought enough *provisionals* with them to last a couple of weeks.

EXERCISE 24C

Rewrite each of the sentences below, replacing the italicized word or phrase with a word from Word List 24 and writing the word in the form that fits the rest of the sentence. Use each word only once. Write your answers in the spaces provided.

1. The leg will be *surgically removed* along the line of the *cut made by the surgeon*.

   . . . .

   . . . .

2. As we *walked leisurely* along the river bank, we admired the *loosely swinging* branches of the willow trees.

   . . . .

   . . . .

3. For engaging in such *unlawful* activities, you could be *locked up* in the state prison for up to five years.

   . . . .

   . . . .

4. Be as *precise and definite* as possible in describing the *distinguishing qualities and characteristics* of these people.

   ....

   ....

5. Supporters of the *temporary* government say that freedom cannot flourish in a country that is *governed by a single leader or political party with complete control.*

   ....

   ....

6. We left the table with a feeling of *having eaten far too much.*

   ....

   ....

7. These *sudden and severe contractions of the muscles* in the chest indicate that the fumes she inhaled are *harmful to health.*

   ....

   ....

8. The car was stuck in the mud and could not be *released from the difficulty it was in.*

   ....

   ....

9. The *bits of sediment at the bottom of the liquid* should be thrown away.

   ....

   ....

EXERCISE 24D

This exercise reviews the roots, prefixes, and suffixes covered in this book.

Give the meanings of the roots italicized in the words below. Give the language from which the root is derived and examples of two other words with the same root.

1. de*scribe*
   meaning: ....

   origin: ....

   examples: ....

2. *tempo*rary
   meaning: ....

   origin: ....

   examples: ....

3. ex*termin*ate
   meaning: ....

   origin: ....

   examples: ....

4. *cred*ulous
   meaning: ....

   origin: ....

   examples: ....

5. ef*fect*ive
   meaning: ....

   origin: ....

   examples: ....

6. bio*graph*y
   meaning: ....

   origin: ....

   examples: ....

7. *uni*verse
   meaning: . . . .

   origin: . . . .

   examples: . . . .

8. *chron*icle
   meaning: . . . .

   origin: . . . .

   examples: . . . .

9. pre*dict*
   meaning: . . . .

   origin: . . . .

   examples: . . . .

10. de*tract*
    meaning: . . . .

    origin: . . . .

    examples: . . . .

Give the meanings of the prefixes italicized in the words below. Give the language from which the prefix is derived and examples of two other words with the same prefix.

11. *trans*fusion
    meaning: . . . .

    origin: . . . .

    examples: . . . .

12. *syn*thetic
    meaning: . . . .

    origin: . . . .

    examples: . . . .

13. *de*vious
    meaning: . . . .

    origin: . . . .

    examples: . . . .

14. *ex*pel
    meaning: . . . .

    origin: . . . .

    examples: . . . .

15. *a*theist
    meaning: . . . .

    origin: . . . .

    examples: . . . .

16. *de*mote
    meaning: . . . .

    origin: . . . .

    examples: . . . .

17. *in*sane
    meaning: . . . .

    origin: . . . .

    examples: . . . .

18. *anti*dote
    meaning: . . . .

    origin: . . . .

    examples: . . . .

19. *a*bed
    meaning: . . . .

    origin: . . . .

    examples: . . . .

20. *ante*date

    meaning: . . . .

    origin: . . . .

    examples: . . . .

Complete the italicized words in the phrases below by adding the appropriate suffix from the following list. Use each suffix only once.

-able	*-ish*
-ary	*-like*
-dom	*-ly*
-eer	*-ment*
-er	*-ness*
-est	*-ren*
-hood	*-ship*
-ile	*-ster*
-ing	*-th*
-ious	*-y*

21. to believe in *free* . . . . of speech

    to speak *free* . . . .

22. a *boy* . . . . smile

    my *boy* . . . . in Indiana

23. a *child* . . . . trust in others

    several *child* . . . .

24. *victor* . . . . in battle

    a glorious *victor* . . . .

25. to be a *grow* . . . . of flowers

    a two-day *grow* . . . . of beard

26. a *volunt* . . . . in the army

    a *volunt* . . . . confession

27. to be *think* . . . . of summer

    an *unthink* . . . . idea

28. the *hard* . . . . of the wood

    to undergo great *hard* . . . .

29. the *young* . . . . member of the group

    a bright *young* . . . eight years old

30. a *frag* . . . . chair

    a *frag* . . . . of bone

EXERCISE 24E

Write out, in the spaces provided, the words from Word List 24 for which a definition, synonym, or antonym is given on the next page. When you are asked to give a root or a prefix, you should refer back to the preceding exercise; the information you require will be found there. Make sure that each of your answers has the same number of letters as there are spaces. A definition followed by a number is a review word; the number gives the Word List from which it is taken.

If all the words are filled in correctly, the boxes running down the answer spaces will conclude the quotation begun in Exercise 23E.

1. to dissolve and wash out (16)

2. to release from some difficulty

3. a sudden, involuntary muscular tightening

4. to remove surgically, as a limb

5. cowardly (18)

6. a distinguishing quality or characteristic

7. a synonym for *definite*

8. sediment in a liquid

9. a synonym for *unlawful*

10. a cut by a surgeon

11. a synonym for *imprison*

12. a person guided and helped by another (23)

13. a synonym for *drooping*

14. showing loftiness of spirit (23)

15. governed by a single leader or political party with complete control

16. a feeling of having had too much

17. emphasizing trivial points of learning (23)

18. to avoid; to shun (10)

19. an antonym for *harmless*

20. temporary; conditional

21. a synonym for *stroll*

WORDLY WISE 24

Don't confuse ILLICIT, which means "unlawful; illegal," with *elicit* (see Word List 2), which means "to draw out; to bring forth" (I managed to *elicit* the information that he was engaged in *illicit* business practices).

NOXIOUS and *obnoxious* are derived from the same Latin root *noxi* (harm) and at one time were identical in meaning. However, in modern usage *noxious* means "injurious to health; harmful," and *obnoxious* has become a milder term meaning "objectionable; offensive."

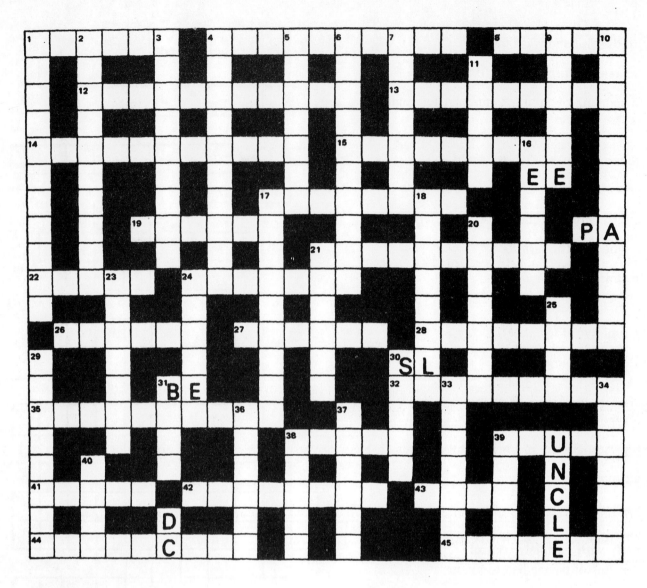

Across

1. a difficult or dangerous situation
4. pity; sympathy
8. a distinctive quality or characteristic
12. showing loftiness of spirit; generous
13. a distinctive feature, as of the face
14. to imprison
15. to include; to enclose
17. emphasizing trivial points of learning
19. threat of force; compulsion
21. to collect gradually; to pile up
22. highly-skilled; expert (6)
24. to deceive into doing something
26. swollen; puffed up
27. a general makeup or layout
28. a cut made by a surgeon
32. swinging freely; drooping
35. the passing off of another's work as one's own
38. the sediment in a liquid
39. to give off
41. to walk leisurely
42. definite; precise
43. a tiny amount
44. to release from some difficulty or danger
45. a feeling of having had too much

Down

1. temporary; conditional
2. perfectly clean and pure; spotless
3. gripping firmly; persistent
4. to act contrary to; to go against
5. a person guided or helped by another
6. that which nourishes or gives strength
7. unlawful; not permitted
9. unwilling; opposed (5)
10. governed by a single leader or party with complete control
11. rate of speed (6)
16. calm and dignified
17. a fictitious or assumed name
18. not moving; motionless
20. soft and flabby
21. the graduates of a college or university (8)
23. an overland route between navigable waterways
24. to pester; to annoy, as with questions
25. an airtight tower for storing fodder (14)
29. to remove surgically; to cut off
30. a sudden muscular contraction
31. to abruptly refuse to act
33. harmful to health; unwholesome
34. to call for particularly (1)
36. to withdraw from a group or organization
37. weak from old age
38. a god or godlike figure
39. to demand
40. to aid in wrongdoing (4)